Becoming a Reflective Educator

Second Edition

CORWIN
PRESS

The Corwin Press logo—a raven striding across an open book—represents the happy union of courage and learning. We are a professional-level publisher of books and journals for K–12 educators, and we are committed to creating and providing resources that embody these qualities. Corwin's motto is "Success for All Learners."

Becoming a Reflective Educator

Second Edition

How to Build a Culture of Inquiry in the Schools

Timothy G. Reagan
Charles W. Case
John W. Brubacher

CORWIN PRESS, INC.
A Sage Publications Company
Thousand Oaks, California

For information:

Corwin Press, Inc.
A Sage Publications Company
2455 Teller Road
Thousand Oaks, California 91320
E-mail: order@corwinpress.com

Sage Publications Ltd.
6 Bonhill Street
London EC2A 4PU
United Kingdom

Sage Publications India Pvt. Ltd.
M-32 Market
Greater Kailash I
New Delhi 110 048 India

Printed in the United States of America

Library of Congress Cataloging-in-Publication Data

Reagan, Timothy G.
    Becoming a reflective educator: How to build a culture
of inquiry in the schools/by Timothy G. Reagan, Charles W. Case,
John W. Brubacher.—2nd ed.
        p.   cm.
    Brubacher's name appears first on the earlier edition.
    Includes bibliographical references and index.
    ISBN 0-7619-7552-7 (cloth: alk. paper)
    ISBN 0-7619-7553-5 (pbk.: alk. paper)
        1. Teaching. 2. Teaching—Case studies. 3. Teachers—
Case studies. 4. School management and organization—
Case studies. 5. Inquiry (Theory of knowledge). I. Case,
Charles W. II. Brubacher, John W. III. Title.
LB1025.3.R424 2000
371.102—dc 21   99-006930

This book is printed on acid-free paper.

05   7   6   5   4

Corwin Editorial Assistant: Catherine Kantor
Production Editor: Denise Santoyo
Editorial Assistant: Victoria Cheng
Typesetter/Designer: Christina M. Hill
Cover Designer: Oscar Desierto
Indexer: Cristina Haley

CONTENTS

PREFACE TO
THE SECOND EDITION

T his new edition of *Becoming a Reflective Educator* is designed for use in teacher education programs that are devoted to the ideal of reflective practice, as well as in advanced courses with experienced educators concerned about becoming more reflective in their teaching. The book, which combines case studies with discussions of various central themes related to teaching, professionalism, and reflective practice, has been carefully constructed to allow it to function as either the central textbook in a general introductory or foundational course in a teacher education program or as a supplementary text in other courses (including the student-teaching experience or advanced, graduate-level course work). Each chapter in *Becoming a Reflective Educator* begins with one or more case studies, which are then analyzed and discussed in terms of the chapter's focus. Finally, each chapter except the last one ends with a series of propositions that is derived from the content of the chapter and that offers points for further reflection and discussion.

Chapter 1 offers a broad overview of the nature and purposes of "reflective practice" as such practice applies to the classroom teacher, as well as an explanation of how reflective practice differs from "good teaching" and an indication of what is entailed in the process of becoming a reflective practitioner. This chapter is central to the remainder of the book and provides its organizing framework.

Chapter 2 provides a general discussion of the role of inquiry in reflective practice; the general point of this chapter is that a necessary component of reflective practice is the ongoing commitment to inquiry, broadly conceived. The concept of inquiry developed in this chapter is based in large part on that discussed by the American philosopher of education John Dewey earlier in this century and is expanded to include various qualitative and naturalistic approaches to inquiry, as well as traditional understandings of what constitutes research. The chapter also seeks to build further on the concept of inquiry by focusing on the ideal of the "teacher as researcher." We argue in this chapter that the reflective analytic teacher must also be a creative and innovative agent in the process of inquiry and, further, that the focus of such inquiry needs to be grounded in real-world problems and concerns that affect classroom teaching and learning. Finally, we emphasize that there is no single approach to research or inquiry and that the reflective practitioner must be open to a wide range and variety of inquiry options.

Chapter 3 offers a broad overview of the role of professional ethics in reflective practice. After several case studies, the chapter presents a discussion of the differences among opinions, preferences, and value judgments and then explores different ethical theories and their implications for teaching practice, as well as the significance of caring for the professional educator. The chapter concludes with a discussion of the role of reflection on ethical professional practice.

Chapter 4 deals with the role of the school in a democratic society, with particular emphasis on the nexus of school and community. The chapter includes discussion of the role of critical pedagogy in teaching practice and the relationship among democratic schooling, critical pedagogy, and reflective practice.

Chapter 5 offers an extended discussion of the nature, purposes, and objectives of both transformative and constructivist curricula and instruction. The theme of this chapter is that the development of transformative curricula and instructional approaches is an essential aspect of reflective practice and must be undertaken in the same manner as other components of reflective practice. The likelihood of resistance to such innovation is also stressed.

Chapter 6 addresses issues of leadership and followership in the school context, with special emphasis on the role of the reflective practitioner as an educational leader and follower. Implications of the themes of reflective practice and the culture of inquiry for school leadership are discussed, and the distinctions between and among different leadership strategies and types of leadership are clarified.

In Chapter 7, we turn our attention to the role of teacher education programs in preparing reflective educators. The chapter begins with examples of several very different approaches to teacher preparation and then identifies some criteria that seem to be necessary for both coherent teacher preparation and effective professional in-service development. In this chapter, we stress that there is no single "right" or "best" kind of teacher education program but that it is nevertheless possible to evaluate and compare different programs.

Finally, Chapter 8 suggests activities that we believe will help individuals become more reflective and analytic professionals.

Becoming a Reflective Educator is the result of more than a decade of collaboration at the University of Connecticut. During the past 15 years, the teacher education program at UConn has been radically transformed from a fairly traditional program, which consisted of a standard collection of courses topped off with a student-teaching experience, to an innovative, 5-year program (2 years in general liberal arts course work, followed by 3 years in the School of Education) that combines university course work, discussion seminars, and clinical and internship experiences throughout the 3 years of the teacher education program. The program is an integrated one in several ways: Not only are university courses, seminars, and clinical experiences closely integrated, but so are the university courses themselves. Further, the program itself is an "integrated bachelor's/master's program." As the faculty, students, and public school constituencies involved in this transformation have worked together to create an exciting and effective teacher education program, we have also reflected on our work and the program and have continued to make changes as appropriate (see Campbell et al., 1995; Case, Norlander, & Reagan, 1995; Norlander, Case, Reagan, Campbell, & Strauch, 1997; Norlander-Case, Reagan, Campbell, & Case, 1998; Norlander-Case, Reagan, & Case, 1999; Reagan, Case, & Norlander, 1993; Reagan, Norlander, Case, & Brubacher, 1994; Schwab & Reagan, in press).

One underlying theme of the UConn teacher education program has been to educate teachers who will themselves be reflective practitioners. This book is the result of extended discussion among the three authors and our colleagues and students about how this could be accomplished. We are especially grateful to Pam Campbell, Tom DeFranco, Eva Díaz, Mary Ann Doyle, Jo Ann Freiberg, Rob Lonning, Judy Meagher, David Moss, Kay Norlander-Case, Terry Osborn, Rich Schwab, Stan Shaw, Cheryl Spaulding, Mary Weinland, and Tim Weinland for their insights, comments, and support. We see this book as a "manual" of sorts to help teacher education students, as well as experienced teachers, develop not only an understanding of the nature of reflective practice but also the attitudes and skills that such an approach to teaching requires.

This second edition has been significantly reorganized on the basis of our own teaching experience and feedback from colleagues all over the United States. It also contains a great deal of new and updated material and reflects many of the changes that have taken place in U.S. public education and society since we wrote the first edition.

This book is our effort to help our students and others become reflective practitioners. We hope it is useful and successful and would, as always, certainly appreciate comments, feedback, and suggestions for changes.

Timothy G. Reagan
Charles W. Case
John W. Brubacher

ABOUT THE AUTHORS

Timothy G. Reagan is Professor of Educational Studies and Foreign Language Education in the Department of Curriculum and Instruction at the University of Connecticut. A former classroom teacher and board of education member, his areas of interest include teacher education, foreign language education, educational linguistics, language education, the education of culturally and linguistically dominated groups, multicultural education, education in non-Western settings, and education of the deaf. He has published extensively, and his work has appeared in such journals as *Harvard Educational Review, Educational Theory, Educational Foundations, Sign Language Studies, Language Problems and Language Planning,* and *Journal of Research and Development in Education.*

Charles W. Case is Professor of Educational Leadership and former Dean of the School of Education at the University of Connecticut. The author of more than 100 books, chapters, and articles dealing with various educational topics, he has actively championed both school reform and the reform of teacher education programs. A former public school teacher, he has also held appointments at the University of Iowa, the University of Wisconsin-Oshkosh, Cleveland State University, and the University of Vermont.

John W. Brubacher is Professor Emeritus of Educational Leadership at the University of Connecticut. For the past 29 years, he has been in the Department of Educational Leadership, where he served for 15 years as Chairperson. Prior to becoming a professor, he was Superintendent of Schools in the Bellevue Public Schools in Bellevue, Washington, and in the Alpena Public Schools in Alpena, Michigan. He has also been an elementary school principal and classroom teacher. He was awarded an A.B. from Yale University; an M.A. from Teachers College, Columbia University; and a Ph.D. from the University of Michigan.

REFLECTION, REFLECTIVE
PRACTICE, AND THE TEACHER

*Too many people think they are thinking when all they
are doing is rearranging their prejudices.*

William James

THE FIRST DAY OF SCHOOL:
THREE CASE STUDIES

The first day of the school year at Emerson Elementary School
was a difficult one for the three new teachers in the building. Sam
Sharp, Doris Gleb, and Amy Gilson had all graduated from Northern State University with good grades and strong recommendations
the year before, and all three, despite the inevitable first-day nerves,
had started the day with high hopes. By the end of the first day of
school, though, each of the three was tired, disappointed, and
depressed.

Sam Sharp's First Day

Sam had been assigned one of the three first-grade classes at
Emerson. He had student-taught in a second-grade class during the
spring semester and had thought he was ready for his own class. In
fact, toward the end of his student-teaching experience, he had found
that he actually preferred to be left alone with the class, rather than
have his cooperating teacher in the room with him. He felt confident

of his ability to handle the class on his own and believed that he was already a very good teacher.

Ten minutes into his first day alone, though, things started going wrong. He had problems with everything from collecting lunch money (with Nicole Jameson's money—mainly in pennies!—spilling all over the place) to repeatedly losing control of the class as the noise and activity levels rose well beyond what he thought were reasonable limits. When he finally got home, he collapsed in a chair and began recounting his horror stories to his girlfriend, Lorna, who listened patiently and tried to be supportive. In retrospect, as he talked about the day's events, Sam began to feel better about the day and to see some humor in it. He even chuckled as he remembered the pennies rolling off in all directions, his own comic efforts to catch them, and the children's roars of laughter. In retrospect, it actually had been fairly funny, he thought to himself. He had lost control early in the day, he realized, and that had set the tone for everything else that happened. The problem, he decided, was that he had been taking himself too seriously. He would do a better job tomorrow, he was sure, and decided that the best thing to do would be to start the day by joking with the class that, after the first day, things had to get better.

Doris Gleb's First Day

Doris also had a long and hard day down the hall, trying to get her sixth graders organized for the school year. Things started out OK but rapidly deteriorated as the students continually tested her authority. By lunchtime, Doris knew she needed to regain control, and so after lunch she threatened to keep the whole class after school if they didn't settle down and get to work. The class not only did not improve but got wilder and more out of control by the hour. By the time the final bell rang, though, Doris didn't have the energy to try to keep the class after school, and in any case, she knew that, with the bus schedules, it wasn't really possible to do so anyway. As she drove home, she became angrier and angrier. The day had been a disaster; there was no doubt about that. But after all, it hadn't really been her fault. Her methods teachers had never taught her how to regain control of a class, and besides, if the students were this bad, the principal should have warned her in advance so that she could be ready for them. She was also irritated that Mrs. Chin, the other sixth-grade teacher, hadn't bothered to come in to see whether she needed any help. It seemed to her that this was the least an experienced teacher could do for a newcomer. After she got home, Doris decided that things at school would eventually work themselves out and that she needed to take her mind off the day. So, she fixed herself a sandwich and turned on the television, looking forward to a quiet and relaxing evening.

Amy Gilson's First Day

Amy arrived at school early so that she could finish getting her classroom set up the way she wanted it. The bulletin boards were colorful and well done and emphasized several themes she planned to focus on with her third graders. The desks were in neat, straight rows, and she had put the textbooks out on each desk. That way, she thought, she could get right down to teaching and not waste any time on setup and classroom organization. As the children arrived, though, they seemed to have other ideas. During the first hour of class, several boys began "accidentally" pushing the piles of books off their desks. This game ended only when Amy actually yelled at Dennis Smith, one instigator of the game—something she had never thought she would have to do to get control of her class. By recess, the neat lines of desks had deteriorated into snakelike rows, and some children had made deliberately circuitous trips to the back of the room to sharpen pencils (and, in the process, had managed to push the desks into even odder and less regular patterns). By the end of the day, Amy had a terrible headache and wondered whether she really wanted to be a teacher after all. Before leaving the school, though, she took 15 minutes to write in the journal she had been keeping since her first field experience in a school while in college. Much to her amazement and chagrin, Amy quickly listed seven major mistakes she thought she had made during the day, and she was fairly sure there were others she'd missed. Next to each mistake, she left room to write in other comments later. She took the journal home with her and, after taking two aspirins and fixing a cup of herbal tea, sat down and reread what she'd written. Then, next to each comment, she added a way of correcting or avoiding each mistake in the future. For instance, next to "Neat rows were a dumb idea; they were like waving a red flag to the kids!" she wrote, "I'm going to put the desks together in groups of four (or maybe six?—I should ask one of the other teachers about this) and see if that helps." She still felt bad about yelling at Dennis, and she promised herself that tomorrow she would make a point of praising him about something. As she got up and closed her journal, she decided that she still wanted to be a teacher but that it was going to be a lot more difficult than she had expected.

Analysis and Discussion. The first-day experiences of Sam, Doris, and Amy are instructive, not because they tell us about good or bad teaching or about such issues as classroom management or instructional strategies, but rather because they provide us with three very different models of how teachers can (and do) reflect on and respond to their classroom experiences. All three of these new teachers had relatively unsuccessful experiences, and all three had to some extent engaged in poor teaching practice. These elements are common not only to Sam, Doris, and Amy but to all teachers. Everyone who has ever entered a classroom as a teacher has had failures, and everyone has made mistakes and, from time to time, made questionable pedagogical judgments and engaged in inappropriate or ineffective teaching practice. There are good teachers and bad teachers, but no perfect teachers. The difference between good teachers and bad teachers often has as much to do with what they do after the fact as it does with what happens in the classroom at a given point in time.

Consider our three novice teachers and how each dealt with his or her failures during the first day. Sam exhibited fairly traditional teacher behavior: He went home and relived the day by recounting to his girlfriend what happened. Spouses of teachers will readily affirm that this is a common behavioral pattern among even the most experienced and successful teachers. At the end of the school day, we want to share our successes ("Crystal Pinkston finally got a perfect score on the spelling test! I'm so proud of the way she's been working!") and to have someone with whom we can commiserate about our failures ("I just can't figure out how to get Harvey to take his work more seriously; I feel like I'm talking to a brick wall sometimes."). In Sam's case, the discussion was obviously fairly successful because he did identify a problem in his own conduct (taking himself too seriously) and worked out a plan of action for correcting the problem.

Doris's response to the day's events was very different from Sam's. She, too, clearly realized that the day had not gone well. Unlike Sam, however, who had accepted his own responsibility for what had taken place in his classroom, Doris chose to blame others. She implicitly blamed the students, categorizing them as "bad kids," and explicitly blamed her college instructors, the principal, and her colleague,

Mrs. Chin. One of the most difficult lessons for many of us to learn is to take responsibility for our own actions and to recognize that we are responsible for whatever takes place in our classrooms. This is a lesson, it would seem, that Doris has not yet learned. Having assigned blame to virtually everyone except herself, Doris then decided that the situation at school would ultimately sort itself out, and so she put it out of her mind. In other words, Doris really did not try to identify what actually went wrong, nor did she develop any plan of action to correct it or to improve the situation in the morning. Because she has not really reflected in a constructive way about what took place in her classroom and because she is expecting things simply to sort themselves out without help, it is unlikely that Doris's teaching will improve without a significant change of attitude and behavior on her part.

Amy, the last of our three novice teachers, had clearly tried to ensure that her first day on the job would be a positive and successful experience. Her day, though, like those of Sam and Doris, had turned out otherwise. In fact, things had gone so badly that she had even lost her temper with a child and yelled at him in class. As she tried to make sense of what had gone wrong, Amy used a process similar to but more formal than that used by Sam: She used a journal to record the major events of the day and then, a bit later, to reflect on those events and develop strategies for dealing with the problems she had identified.

The responses of these three new teachers can be categorized as falling along a *continuum of reflectivity*; that is, the ways Sam, Doris, and Amy responded to their first day on the job demonstrate different degrees and kinds of reflection. Doris, in effect, refused to reflect critically on the day's events at all, exhibiting essentially nonreflective behavior. Sam did reflect on the day's events and, on the basis of his reflection, devised a strategy for correcting or at least improving the situation. His reflection was informal, though, and might more accurately be described as a combination of emoting about how he felt and thinking about what had happened. Finally, Amy's response to her first day of teaching entailed active and deliberate reflection, which included both a brief written description of the day's major events and a critical analysis of and reflection on those events, which in turn led her to formulate strategies for changing her behavior in the classroom. In other words, Amy's reflection was far more formal and elaborate than that of Sam and, as a consequence, may in the long run prove to be more useful and effective.

The cases of Sam, Doris, and Amy are useful in helping us begin to conceptualize the nature and manifestations of reflective practice, but they all focus solely on the emergence of reflective practice on the part of *new* teachers. What about *experienced* classroom teachers? As teachers develop an experiential base, they are able to become reflective in ways (and perhaps about things) that a new teacher is not. We now turn to four case studies that provide examples of reflection and reflective practice in the world of experienced classroom teachers.

THE COMPLEXITIES OF TEACHING: FOUR CASE STUDIES

Rethinking the Content of U.S. History

Mary O'Reilly has taught social studies at Shepstone High School for 4 years. She has always considered herself a good teacher and has had relatively few problems in the past. This year, though, has been different, in large part, Mary believes, because of the presence of the many African American students who have been bused in to previously all-white Shepstone High as part of the court-ordered desegregation of the city. Especially troublesome for Mary has been her third-period U.S. history class. The third-period class consists of students in the vocational track at Shepstone High and includes 12 of the bused students out of the total enrollment of 25. Although she has covered exactly the same material in this class as in her other three U.S. history classes and has tried to do so in the same way in each class, students in the third-period class have consistently done less well on their quizzes and exams than the students in her other classes. Furthermore, 11 of the 12 African American students have been in the D to F grade range throughout the year. On a Friday in early December, a week before the scheduled midterm examination, students in the third-period class, led by Larry Jones, a tall African American student who seemed to have gained the respect of the other vocational students throughout the school, rebelled during class. They complained that the textbook was too difficult, that the class was boring and irrelevant, and that Mary was a racist who was only interested in "what a bunch of old, dead white people said and did." Taken aback by the challenge to her authority, Mary quickly recovered her poise and said she would think over what the class had said. To fill up the remainder of the period, rather than return to the lecture she had planned for the day, she asked each student in the class to take out a sheet of paper and to write down three things, relevant to a class in U.S. history, that he or she would like to learn about. She collected the papers at the end of the period and, unsure of what she should do, watched the students head off for their next class.

In the teachers' lounge during her free period, Mary shared what had happened with Jim Bender, one of the vocational education teachers at Shepstone. Jim shook his head and commented that Larry Jones was a troublemaker and that what Mary needed to do was to regain control of the class on Monday and remind the students who was in charge. After all, he pointed out, it was Mary's job as a teacher to decide what was relevant and important for students to learn. As Jim got up to leave, he turned and said, "Actually, none of this should surprise any of us; what did we think would happen, once they started busing those black kids in here? They should've left well enough alone!"

At home that night, as Mary thought about what had taken place during third period and about Jim's comments, she decided that even though it would be easier to blame the students and busing, maybe Larry and the others did have a point. She'd always assumed that every U.S. history class should basically be interchangeable with every other U.S. history class, but perhaps that wasn't really good teaching. If she could find ways to get students more excited about U.S. history, they would work harder and end up learning more; that just made sense. And, if that meant including material about African Americans in U.S. history, then so be it. Mary realized, however, that she didn't really know anything about African American history or, for that matter, any perspectives on U.S. history other than the ones she had learned as a student in college. She decided that it was about time for her to fill in some of the gaps in her knowledge and figured that she could use the questions the students had given her in class as a starting point. She could go to the public library on Saturday and get some basic material on African American history, she figured, and early next week she could call her college adviser and ask whether he could offer any additional suggestions.

Mary pulled the papers out of her third-period folder and began to look them over, although not with much real hope; this class had been such a disappointment all year, after all. Much to her surprise, the questions were, for the most part, serious ones and raised some important historical questions that demonstrated a far better understanding of what they'd covered in class than Mary had expected. As she read over the questions the students had written for her, she reached a decision. Monday in class she would praise the students for raising the issues with her and for their thoughtful questions as well. She would admit to not knowing much about African American history and ask her students to help her learn more; they would try to work together to discover what none of them knew. At that point, Mary got out a pad of paper and began sketching a timeline and identifying objectives for the rest of the school year, excited and looking forward to Monday's third-period class more than she had since the start of the year.

Reporting a Colleague

Jeremy Butler had been a mathematics teacher at Eastmoor Junior High School since the Dark Ages, or at least so the students believed. Actually, he'd come to Eastmoor 17 years ago, straight out of college, and had become a popular and well-respected teacher in the district. New teachers were especially fond of him because he was always free to provide information and insights about the students; their families, problems, and backgrounds; the town; and the often mysterious workings of the school system. All in all, Jeremy was satisfied with his life and happy to let things continue as they always had, at least until Adrian Gregg joined the faculty as an English teacher.

Adrian had come to the district from the military, having served a hitch after college as an army officer, but he showed no signs of a "military" approach to teaching. He was open, relaxed, and friendly, and the students clearly loved him. He also appeared to be a very effective classroom teacher because the students were continually talking about his classes and about how much they enjoyed what they were studying. By winter vacation, it was difficult to believe that Adrian hadn't been around for years, and Jeremy, like most of the faculty at Eastmoor, was delighted to have Adrian as a colleague.

During winter vacation, Jeremy went out for a drink with friends to a local bar. He saw Adrian across the room and went over to greet him. Adrian had clearly had a bit too much to drink but was delighted to see Jeremy, and they chatted pleasantly about their respective vacation plans. Jeremy thought nothing of the chance encounter until one day in early February when he stopped by Adrian's classroom early in the morning to drop off a notice about a forthcoming union meeting. Adrian wasn't in the room, so Jeremy went over to his desk and put the notice on it. As he was turning to leave, Jeremy noticed that underneath the desk was a half-full bottle of Scotch. Not wishing to intrude on Adrian's privacy or to jump to unwarranted conclusions, Jeremy quickly left the room and decided not to mention to anyone what he'd seen. As the day progressed, though, Jeremy became increasing concerned about what he had seen. If the bottle of Scotch was Adrian's, then it would suggest that perhaps Adrian had a drinking problem and that he needed help. Besides, if something were to happen to a student in one of Adrian's classes because Adrian wasn't fully sober, Jeremy knew that he would never forgive himself. If, however, the principal were to find out about Adrian having the bottle on the premises, let alone any suspicions about alcoholism, that would mean the end of a promising teaching career. Eastmoor was a conservative community, and a new teacher with a drinking problem would have virtually no chance of having his contract renewed; he might even be fired outright. Furthermore, Jeremy knew it was district policy that any suspicions about conduct on the part of a teacher that might endanger students were to be reported without delay to the school principal. Under the circumstances, if he did not report what he had seen, he himself might be at risk. At the same time, he didn't actually know that the bottle of Scotch was Adrian's; for all he knew, Adrian might have taken it from a student. What should he do?

After mentally weighing the pros and cons of the situation for several hours at home that night, Jeremy finally picked up the telephone and called Adrian at home. Adrian answered, sounding less than coherent. Jeremy told Adrian that he needed to speak with him about a personal matter and asked Adrian to stop by his classroom after school the next day. Adrian agreed and showed up at Jeremy's classroom door right on schedule. Jeremy asked Adrian to sit down, told him about accidentally seeing the Scotch bottle, and shared his concerns that Adrian might have a serious drinking problem. Adrian admitted that he drank heavily and that the bottle Jeremy had seen was his, but he denied having a real drinking problem. He promised not to bring liquor into the school again, which he agreed had been a terrible mistake, and begged Jeremy not to report him. Jeremy asked Adrian at least to attend one meeting of Alcoholics Anonymous, but Adrian refused, arguing again that he really didn't have a problem; he also mentioned that Eastmoor was a small town and that if he attended an AA meeting, word would get out and his career would be in jeopardy. Jeremy told Adrian that he'd think about the situation and let him know first thing in the morning what he had decided to do.

It was the most difficult decision Jeremy had had to make since becoming a teacher at Eastmoor. He really liked Adrian and believed that the man was potentially an outstanding teacher. He also believed that Adrian was aware and frightened of the implications of his conduct and thought that perhaps the concern for losing his job might lead to Adrian addressing his drinking. Jeremy didn't want to be responsible for the possibility that Adrian might be fired, which he thought was a probable outcome, given what he knew about the school system. However, Jeremy did recognize in Adrian's denial one of the classic behaviors of the alcoholic and wondered whether Adrian could deal with his problem without professional help. Finally, Jeremy decided that his professional obligations to the students, to the district, and even to Adrian required that he discuss the matter with the school principal. He also decided, though, that he would make a strong case for retaining Adrian as long as he agreed to get professional help. After all his years in the system, Jeremy felt fairly certain that the principal would listen to him. It was the best he could do, Jeremy decided sadly.

Whose Language Is It, Anyhow?

Shelly Svenson had loved the Spanish language from the time she had first begun studying it in eighth grade. She had done exceptionally well throughout high school in the language, and her teachers had encouraged her to consider becoming a foreign language teacher. So, Shelly majored in Spanish in college, spent a year studying in Spain, and then came back and became a Spanish teacher at Rivertown High School.

Shelly had taught at Rivertown for 6 years and was proud of her ability to inspire the same love for the language in her students as she herself felt. Teaching a range of classes, from beginning Spanish through an advanced placement course, Shelly worked hard and expected her students to do likewise. She maintained high standards both for herself and for her students, and as a result she was known throughout the school as a fair but tough teacher. This was, in her view, what good teaching was all about.

Although in the past Shelly generally has not experienced class-room management problems, this has changed in recent years, and the current year is becoming an exceptional one in this regard—and a very trying exception, at that. Two situations are creating problems for her and seem to be getting worse as the year progresses.

The first problem, in Shelly's view, is a change in student place-ments at Rivertown High School. In the past, foreign language courses at Rivertown have been largely populated by college-bound students who needed at least 2 years of a foreign language to get into the state university. Although not all of these students had been enthusiastic language learners, they did, for the most part, do what was expected of them without too much trouble. On her arrival at Rivertown High 3 years ago, though, the new principal of Rivertown took the position that foreign language study is beneficial for every-one and encouraged all students to enroll in a foreign language. Although Shelly appreciates the support for foreign language learn-ing, she has found that many of her students do not behave or respond the way her students in the past had responded. She has grown increasingly frustrated trying to get students to complete homework, to study, and even to participate at a minimal level in class. Her dis-cussions with other foreign language teachers at Rivertown have led her to believe that she is not alone in these problems and that the change of student population in the foreign language classes has had a detrimental effect on the quality of student learning.

The second problem that Shelly is trying to deal with involves a single student, Jorge Díaz. Jorge is Puerto Rican, and at home his fam-ily speaks both English and Spanish. He originally signed up for beginning Spanish, expecting the class to be an "easy A," but he was moved on the recommendation of another Spanish teacher to Shelly's first-period Spanish III class. Jorge does speak Spanish, but not, in Shelly's view, very good Spanish. Among the errors that Shelly has noted in Jorge's speech are misuses of Spanish words (e.g., using the Spanish word *carpeta*, which in Standard Spanish means "a loose-leaf binder," for *carpet*), using English words in place of Spanish words (e.g., using *bil*, rather than *cuenta*, for *bill*; using *troca*, rather than *camión*, for *truck*), using English word order rather than Spanish word order (as in *¿Qué usted piensa?* for *¿Qué piensa usted?*), and many other mistakes. Shelly has worked hard to help Jorge improve his Spanish, but he has resisted her efforts and has grown increasingly hostile in class.

The combination of these two problems has made the year a difficult one for Shelly, and the two problems finally came to a head in class one morning in mid-February. Shelly had planned a review session in preparation for an upcoming exam in Spanish III and began the class by going over a homework sheet she had handed out the day before. She was irritated to discover that only a few students had bothered to do any of the sheet and that several had lost it completely. Shelly decided that it was time to put an end to such behavior and began to lecture the class about their responsibilities and how important it was that they do the assigned homework. In the midst of this, Jorge commented, "Yeah, well, it's not like we're learning real Spanish. What you're teaching isn't what folks all over the place here actually speak! You just want us to learn your Anglo Spanish."

Rather than allow herself to lose control of her class, Shelly simply answered, "What I'm teaching you is good Spanish, and you'll either learn it properly or fail." She then told the students that they were to spend the rest of the period quietly preparing for the exam on their own and that, under the circumstances, she thought there might well be a lot of failing grades.

After class, Shelly used her planning period to sit down with the assistant principal and discuss what had happened. She was angry that a student would challenge her the way Jorge had and was also irritated that her students were simply not doing their part in the learning process. The assistant principal, who had been a mathematics teacher before moving into administration and whom Shelly liked and trusted, advised her that she needed to maintain her standards and that if it meant failing large numbers of students, the administration would, of course, support her. As for Jorge, he commented, "That'll teach him not to try to beat the system; he shouldn't assume that just because he speaks some kind of Spanish at home, learning real Spanish in school will be easy!"

A Case of Child Abuse?

Juan Rodriguez was an experienced, skilled teacher who, after teaching fifth grade at West Springfield Elementary School for 7 years, still found it as exciting and challenging as he had when he first student-taught. He enjoyed his time in the classroom and thought he was having a positive effect on his students' development. He considered himself a good teacher and role model for his students and was confident that others in the school saw him as a caring and competent professional educator. The year had gone well, Juan thought to himself one morning in April as he watched his students working in small groups throughout the room on their social studies projects. Then he noticed the bruises on the back of Jennifer Gordon's left leg. Jennifer had become one of Juan's favorite students; bright, articulate, and attractive, she was a friendly and outgoing girl whose mother was actively involved in the school PTO, as well as a variety of local community groups, and was well known and liked by many of the school faculty. Juan had had no reason to suspect any problems in Jennifer's home life but thought that, in keeping with the school district's policy of reporting all cases of child abuse, he really did need to find out how Jennifer had gotten the bruises. Not wishing to create a disturbance or to upset Jennifer, Juan waited until recess and, while outside on the playground with the children, caught her attention and engaged her in conversation. Jennifer seemed to be very nervous about answering Juan's questions about the bruises and quickly responded that she had fallen off her bicycle. Sensing her nervousness, Juan dropped the subject and let her return to play with the other children. He had, he realized, a real moral dilemma: Reporting a case of suspected child abuse automatically involved the police, and the Gordons were respected citizens in the community. He really didn't have any hard evidence, and although Jennifer was clearly nervous about discussing the bruises, that didn't necessarily mean she'd been physically harmed by her parents. She could be nervous because she had been doing something she wasn't supposed to do or perhaps just because he was a male. Juan decided to give the matter some thought before he did anything, and he went home that night with the issue unresolved.

Juan arrived at school early the next morning, hoping to see Beverly Clark, the reading consultant for the district and a good friend. Beverly was in the office, picking up her mail, and greeted Juan with a ready smile. When he asked her to come down to his classroom to "talk something over," she agreed to come at once and followed him down the hall to his room. Juan shared with Beverly what he had seen the day before and told her about Jennifer's reaction to his questions. Beverly, too, thought that Jennifer's nervousness sounded odd, but she also knew the family's reputation and found it difficult to believe that Jennifer's parents could be guilty of child abuse. After talking it over together, the two decided that the best thing to do was to take it slow and easy and just to observe Jennifer more closely for the next few weeks to see whether anything else suspicious took place. After all, children get bruises all the time, they agreed, and Jennifer's home life was by all accounts a good one. It would be a terrible thing for good parents to be accused of child abuse if they weren't guilty. Juan felt much better as Beverly left, although he wasn't positive that they'd really made the right decision.

Analysis and Discussion. The four case studies you have just read present us with somewhat more difficult and complex examples of the kinds of dilemmas and problems inevitably faced by classroom teachers. Although dealing with very different kinds of issues, each of the experienced classroom teachers demonstrates some similar characteristics and behaviors. Although one may disagree with the conclusions that each teacher reached or with aspects of his or her behavior in the situation, it is nevertheless clear that all four teachers were, in fact, attempting to engage in reflective practice.

In the case of Mary O'Reilly's third-period U.S. history class, students explicitly challenge the content of the curriculum and implicitly challenge the teaching methods the teacher has been employing. Mary's experience as a classroom teacher can be seen clearly in her ability to defuse temporarily the tense classroom situation, as well as in her willingness to jettison her planned lesson in favor of a more appropriate alternative in the class. After class, Mary discusses the situation with a colleague, although his advice, most of us would agree, is poor, if not absolutely reprehensible. Fortunately, on reflection, Mary appears to agree with this assessment and, after a difficult but useful self-critique, decides to admit that her students' concerns are legitimate and to attempt to develop and implement a plan designed to address the students' complaints. Throughout the experience, Mary tries to take her students and their concerns seriously, although there is also an element of paternalism in her responses. Mary could be faulted for not realizing the biased nature of the curriculum on her own, of course, and she still has not realized that her teaching methods, as well as the content she is teaching, may be problematic. In short, this case demonstrates reflective practice related to such issues as curriculum and diversity on the part of an experienced classroom teacher, although we may have reservations or concerns about whether the practice exemplified actually constitutes "good" teaching. What is clear, though, is that Mary will continue to struggle and to try to improve her teaching.

The case of Jeremy Butler and Adrian Gregg focuses, not on classroom practice, but rather on professional ethics and on the educator's responsibility for and toward other professional educators, as well as toward the school district and children served by the district. The decision that Jeremy Butler is called on by circumstances to make is a difficult one, and the reader may well disagree with the decision he finally makes. As with Mary, however, what we see in Jeremy's behavior is a thoughtful, reasoned effort to reach a good judgment about what action he should take in the matter. We see him weighing the evidence and considering the situation in the light of both its moral and practical consequences. It is clear that Jeremy cares deeply about both what happens to Adrian and what is best for the students. It is also interesting to note that Jeremy does not take what for many would be the easy way out: simply reporting his suspicions because the rules require it. Ethical behavior, whether personal or professional, requires that we do more than merely follow the rules blindly and unthinkingly, and Jeremy clearly understands this. Perhaps because of the nature of the situation, however, Jeremy seeks to make his decision in a vacuum, without discussing his options with anyone else. The result is that he takes on far more personal responsibility in the matter than he really needs to, and he may fail to identify other options that are available to him in dealing with the problem of Adrian's drinking.

In the case of Shelly Svenson, several important pedagogical issues are at stake, most related either directly or indirectly to matters concerned with student diversity and how one should deal with such diversity. These questions are becoming increasingly important, not just in foreign language education but in all areas, especially as inclusive education becomes more popular and more commonplace in U.S. education. Shelly has observed significant changes in the students in her classes but seems to have assumed that no changes in her teaching are required; the problem, in her view, is entirely with the students. To some extent, then, Shelly is taking a position that is not too dissimilar from that taken by Doris Gleb. In addition, Shelly's view of "good" or "proper" Spanish, as well as of the variety of Spanish spoken by Jorge, though not uncommon, has been widely rejected by both linguists and language educators (see Fishman & Keller, 1982; Hernandez-Chavez, Cohen, & Beltramo, 1975; Osborn & Reagan, 1998; Reagan &

Osborn, 1998; Valdés, Lozano, & García-Moya, 1981). This having been said, it is also true that Shelly has, on at least two occasions, discussed with colleagues some issues that are bothering her and does seem to take action on professional feedback—however much we might disagree with both her practices and the advice she has received.

The case of Juan Rodriguez and Jennifer Gordon will be, for many of us, the most difficult of these four case studies to address. By virtue of our training, our predispositions, and our lifestyles, on the one hand, good teachers generally tend to like and enjoy children and would not want to contribute to child abuse even indirectly. On the other hand, we are also sensitive to the harm that a false charge of child abuse can cause. As in the case of Adrian Gregg, at times experienced teachers are likely to bend or break school rules, violate district policies, and even break laws when their judgment is that doing so is the "right" thing to do. In this case, after trying (perhaps unsuccessfully) to find out from Jennifer what had happened and discussing the situation with a colleague, Juan decides not to report his suspicions. He has tried to weigh the evidence and his concerns, and he is obviously interested in protecting Jennifer. It is also evident that both Juan and Beverly will now be attentive to any other indications of possible child abuse in Jennifer's case. Both Juan and Beverly, however, seem to have been somewhat inhibited by the social standing of Jennifer's parents; it is not at all clear that Juan would have reached the same conclusion had another child with less well-known parents been involved.

The characteristic that seems to hold all four of these case studies together is that, in each instance, the teacher demonstrated an awareness of and concern with what Thomas Green calls the "conscience of craft" (Green, 1985, pp. 4-7). In a discussion of the formation of individual conscience (of moral development) in contemporary society, Green suggests the following:

> There is such a thing as the conscience of craft. We see it whenever the expert or the novice in any craft adopts the standards of that craft as his or her own. In other words, it is displayed whenever we become judge in our own case, saying that our performance is good or bad, skillful, fitting, or the like. . . Thus, to possess a conscience of craft is to have acquired the capacity for self-congratulation or deep self-satisfaction at something well

done, shame at slovenly work, and even embarrassment at care-lessness. (p. 4)

In each case, the teacher was faced with a dilemma that he or she needed to resolve. Each dilemma required that the teacher use both professional knowledge (whether about the curriculum, professional ethics, or indicators of child abuse) together with rational deci-sion-making skills to make a judgment about and take action in response to the dilemma. Although one may have serious reserva-tions (or even disagreements) with the decisions reached and actions taken by the four teachers in these cases, it is clear that each did his or her best to comply with Green's notion of the "conscience of craft" and, further, that each individual, regardless of the rightness or wrongness of the decision, only decided what to do after careful, thoughtful reflection. With these seven case studies in mind, we can now turn to a more detailed discussion of what is actually entailed in *reflective practice* and why such reflective practice is a desirable goal for the classroom teacher.

THE NATURE OF REFLECTIVE PRACTICE

A perennial debate among educators and those interested in education has developed about the nature of teaching. The debate is most commonly presented as a dichotomy, with the basic issue being defined as whether teaching is best understood as an artistic endeavor, with the teacher's role seen as roughly comparable to that of a painter or creative writer, or whether teaching is best conceptu-alized as a sort of "science," consisting of a collection of technical skills, with the teacher's role seen as having more in common with that of a medical technician or an automobile mechanic (see Barzun, 1954, 1991; Gage, 1978, 1985; Highet, 1950). At first glance, the debate appears to be an important one because the way we concep-tualize teaching has a great deal to do with whether teachers are seen (and rewarded) as professionals such as doctors, lawyers, engi-neers, and the like, as well as with how teachers can best be prepared (can good teachers be made, or are they just "born," as the old adage goes?). Writing in defense of the artistic view of the teacher, for instance, Mark Van Doren (1959) has commented:

Good teachers have always been and will always be, and there are good teachers now. The necessity henceforth is that fewer of them be accidents. The area of accident is reduced when there is a design which includes the education of teachers. Not the training—a contemporary term that suggests lubricating oil and precision parts, not to say reflexes and responses. (pp. 170-171)

Although the debate between those who see teaching as basically an art form that is largely instinctive in good teachers and those who see it as a scientific set of technical skills that virtually anyone, properly motivated, can acquire is a fascinating one to listen to and think about, it is also misleading, much as the nature-nurture debate is misleading. It is misleading because experienced educators know that teaching entails many elements of both artistic sensitivity and technical skill and that good teaching practice is impossible without both types of elements. It is interesting to note that one could make precisely this same claim for the competent practice of virtually all professions. For example, if one considers what a physician actually does, one finds a combination of technical skills and knowledge and of professional "instinct" that is, in essence, artistic in nature, which is remarkably similar to that exhibited by teachers. An excellent illustration of this point is provided in *Newton's Madness: Further Tales of Clinical Neurology* (Kalwans, 1990), a collection of case studies by a noted neurologist, that reads more like a detective novel than a medical work. The underlying theme in *Newton's Madness* is that medical diagnosis is actually far less scientific (at least in a narrow, positivistic sense) than most of us usually assume. The medical education a physician receives is intended to help him or her identify possible diagnoses and to eliminate others, but very often the final diagnosis in any particular case depends to a considerable extent on judgment calls. This point was clearly recognized in the 1984 GPEP report of the Association of American Medical Colleges entitled *Physicians for the Twenty-First Century*, which, according to medical historian Kenneth Ludmerer, presented this conclusion: "[M]edical education should prepare students 'to learn throughout their professional lives rather than simply to master current information and techniques.' To accomplish this, students must be active, independent learners and problem solvers rather than passible recipients of information" (Ludmerer, 1985, p. 264). Furthermore, critics of modern U.S. medical practice often note that where technical competence is removed from ethical and humanitarian concerns, what is left is essentially poor medical practice and treatment (e.g., see Jones, 1981). As Paul Starr (1982) has noted,

> In its commitment to the preservation of life, medical care ironically has come to symbolize a prototypically modern form of torture, combining benevolence, indifference, and technical wizardry. Rather than engendering trust, technological medicine often raises anxieties about the ability of individuals to make choices for themselves. (p. 390)

It is the need to make such judgment calls that will, at least for the immediate future, limit the usefulness of computer diagnosis, for instance, because the computer can only perform the technical aspects of the physician's task. The artistic functions continue to require a human presence. The same is true for other professions as well (see Case, Lanier, & Miskel, 1986; Schön, 1983, 1987; for an interesting and relevant discussion of the training of attorneys, see Stevens, 1983) and is certainly true in the case of teaching. An interesting point here is that Ivan Illich, who is perhaps best known for the criticism of compulsory schooling he offered in *Deschooling Society* (1970), has also critiqued contemporary medical practice in roughly the same manner, in large part on the basis of similarities of the medical and educational establishments (see Illich, 1975; Reagan, 1980).

Much of the daily work of the classroom teacher actually involves making judgments and decisions, often with limited information. Rather than think about the role of the teacher in terms of whether teaching is best understood as an art form, a set of technical skills, or some combination of these two extremes, we suggest that teaching can be more accurately and usefully conceptualized in terms of the role of the teacher as decision maker. Consider, for a moment, the many different kinds of judgments and decisions the typical teacher engages in during his or her normal, daily routine. The teacher makes curricular decisions, methodological decisions, decisions about individual children and their needs and problems, decisions about classroom management and organization, decisions about both personal and professional ethics, and so on. The philosopher of education Robert Fitzgibbons (1981) has suggested that teachers make decisions of three types: (a) those concerned basically with *educational outcomes* (with what the goals or results of the educational experience should be), (b) those concerned with the *matter of education* (with what is, could be, or should be taught), and (c) those concerned with the *manner of education* (with how teaching should take place) (pp. 13-14).

When a teacher makes a decision, he or she is doing far more than merely taking a course of action or acting in a certain way. The process of decision making should be a rational one, which means the teacher (whether consciously or unconsciously) considers and weighs alternatives and employs criteria to select a given option or course of action. Unfortunately, as Jere Brophy has reported, "[M]ost studies of teachers' interactive decision-making portray it as more reactive than reflective, more intuitive than rational, and more routinized than conscious" (as quoted in Irwin, 1987, p. 1). Good teaching, however, requires reflective, rational, and conscious decision making. As Charles E. Silberman has argued in *Crisis in the Classroom* (1971), "We must find ways of stimulating public school teachers . . . to think about what they are doing and why they are doing it" (p. 380). An important element in this process of reflective, rational, and conscious decision making is that we can reasonably expect a teacher to be able to justify his or her decisions and actions in the classroom. Justification of decisions and actions, as Cornel Hamm (1989) explains, is actually a fairly simple and straightforward matter: "To provide a justification for a course of action is to provide good reasons or grounds for that course of action" (p. 163).

To be able to provide such justification, the teacher cannot rely either on instinct alone or on prepackaged sets of techniques. Instead, he or she must think about what is taking place, what the options are, and so on, in a critical, analytic way. In other words, the teacher must engage in *reflection* about his or her practice, just as the physician must reflect about the symptoms and other evidence presented by a patient. The idea of the teacher as reflective practitioner is not a new one; John Dewey, the noted American philosopher of education, wrote about the need for reflective thinking as early as 1903 and dealt with the role of reflection extensively in both *How We Think* (1910, 1933) and *Logic: The Theory of Inquiry* (1938). For Dewey, logical theory and analysis was a generalization of the reflective process in which we all engage from time to time. Dewey recognized that we can "reflect" on a whole host of things in the sense of merely "thinking about" them; however, logical, or *analytic*, reflection can take place only when there is a real problem to be solved. As Dewey (1903/1976) explained,

The general theory of reflection, as over against its concrete exercise, appears when occasions for reflection are so over-whelming and so mutually conflicting that specific adequate response in thought is blocked. Again, it shows itself when prac-tical affairs are so multifarious, complicated, and remote from control that thinking is held off from successful passage into them. (p. 300)

For Dewey, then, true reflective practice takes place only when the individual is faced with a real problem that he or she needs to resolve and seeks to resolve that problem in a rational manner. All three of the new teachers discussed were faced with problems they believed to be quite real and of considerable personal interest; both Sam and Amy engaged (though to different degrees and in different ways) in what Dewey would see as reflection.

Recent emphasis on the need for reflective practice comes largely from the work of Donald Schön (1983, 1987), which has been widely used by educators and others interested in the preparation of class-room teachers. Such concerns with reflective practice are also tied very closely to efforts to empower teachers, as Catherine Fosnot (1989) has noted: "An empowered teacher is a reflective decision maker who finds joy in learning and in investigating the teach-ing/learning process—one who views learning as construction and teaching as a facilitating process to enhance and enrich development" (p. xi).

Several ways of conceptualizing reflective practice as it applies to the activities of classroom teachers have been suggested in recent years. A good place to begin a discussion of reflective practice is with the distinction among the three types of reflection that Killion and Todnem (1991), using Schön's (1983) earlier work as a base, have sug-gested. According to Killion and Todnem, we can distinguish among *reflection-on-action, reflection-in-action,* and *reflection-for-action* (p. 15). Both reflection-in-action and reflection-on-action are essentially reac-tive in nature, being distinguished primarily by *when* reflection takes place—with reflection-in-action referring to reflection in the midst of practice (as in the case of Mary O'Reilly's change in her day's lesson as a result of her students' actions, or in the case of Juan Rodriguez seek-ing information from Jennifer about her bruises), and reflection-on-practice referring to reflection that takes place after an event. Reflec-tion-for-action, in contrast, as Killion and Todnem argue, is the desired outcome of both previous types of reflection. We undertake reflection, not so much to revisit the past or to become aware of the metacognitive process one is experiencing (both noble reasons in themselves), but to guide future action (the more practical purpose). (p. 15)

In other words, reflection-for-practice is proactive in nature. Examples of reflection-for-practice can be found in almost every case study presented in this chapter; only in the case of Doris Gleb is there no indication of reflection-for-practice. To sum up, it is clear that all three types of reflection discussed here will be necessary components of reflective practice on the part of the classroom teacher. Having said this, it is also important for us to note here that the relative significance of each of these three components of reflective practice may change during an individual teacher's career; thus, for the novice teacher, reflection-for-practice and reflection-on-practice may be the most obvious ways in which his or her practice is distinguished, whereas for the expert or master teacher, reflectivity may be best seen in his or her reflection-in-practice. Further, the process of engaging in reflection-for-practice should be seen, not as a linear one, but as an ongoing spiral in which each element of reflective practice is constantly involved in an interactive process of change and development.

Van Manen (1977) has suggested a hierarchical model of *levels of reflectivity*. According to Van Manen, three distinct levels of reflective practice can be seen, at least ideally, as paralleling the growth of the individual teacher from novice to expert or master teacher. The first level is concerned with the effective application of skills and technical knowledge in the classroom setting. At this first level, reflection entails only the appropriate selection and use of instructional strategies and the like in the classroom. The second level involves reflection about the assumptions underlying specific classroom practices, as well as about the consequences of particular strategies, curricula, and so on. In other words, at the second level of reflectivity, teachers begin to apply educational criteria to teaching practice to make individual and independent decisions about pedagogical matters. Finally, the third level of reflectivity (sometimes called *critical reflection*) entails the questioning of moral, ethical, and other types of normative criteria related directly and indirectly to the classroom (see Irwin, 1996). Judith Irwin (1987) explains:

This includes concern for justice, equity and the satisfaction of important human purposes within the larger social context. A teacher engaging in this level of reflection, then, would be able to not only make decisions which would be beneficial for the long-term development of the students in that classroom but also to contribute to educational policy beyond his/her individual classroom. (p. 5)

Another approach to conceptualizing reflective practice is not to view such practice in a hierarchical manner, but rather to focus instead on elements that appear to play significant roles in fostering reflection and reflective practice on the part of classroom teachers. Georgea Sparks-Langer and Amy Colton (1991), for instance, in a synthesis of the research on teachers' reflective thinking, argue for three such elements: the cognitive element, the critical element, and the narrative element. The *cognitive element* of reflective thinking is concerned with the knowledge that teachers need in order to make good decisions in and about the classroom situation. Lee Shulman (1987) has identified seven broad categories of knowledge that would, taken together, constitute the major categories of the knowledge base for a classroom teacher and that are therefore necessary for successful, reflective teaching practice:

1. Content knowledge
2. General pedagogical knowledge, with special reference to those broad principles and strategies of classroom management and organization that appear to transcend subject matter
3. Curriculum knowledge, with particular grasp of the materials and programs that serve as "tools of the trade" for teachers
4. Pedagogical content knowledge, that special amalgam of content and pedagogy that is uniquely the province of teachers, their own special form of professional understanding
5. Knowledge of learners and their characteristics
6. Knowledge of educational contexts, as diverse as the workings of the group or classroom, the governance and financing of school districts, and the character of communities and cultures
7. Knowledge of educational ends, purposes, and values and their philosophical and historical grounds

It is important to note that although all teachers, whether novice or expert, will have similar bodies of knowledge at their disposal, the organization and structuring of this knowledge may differ radically. Research conducted by cognitive psychologists has suggested that the *schemata*, or organized networks of facts, concepts, generaliza-tions, and experiences, of beginning and experienced teachers are very different in significant ways (Berliner, 1986; see especially Sparks-Langer & Colton, 1991, pp. 37-38). Because such schemata are constructed by teachers over time as a result of their experiences, it is not surprising that experienced teachers will often be able to make sense of and respond to a given problematic situation in the class-room more quickly and effectively than novices. Studies suggesting that expert teachers are able to deal with changes in lesson plans and problematic classroom situations far more successfully than are new teachers can be explained, according to Sparks-Langer and Colton (1991), "because (1) many of the routines and the content were avail-able [to the expert teachers] in memory as automatic scripts and (2) their rich schemata allowed the experts to quickly consider cues in the environment and access appropriate strategies" (p. 38). Schemata of the sort discussed here are constructed naturally over time, but their development can be encouraged and supported by reflective practice. In other words, although good teaching practice does indeed depend on a strong experiential base, reflective practice can help us speed up the development of such an experiential base in new teachers.

The second element of reflective thinking is the *critical element*, which is concerned with "the moral and ethical aspects of social com-passion and justice" (Sparks-Langer & Colton, 1991, p. 39). Issues of social justice and ethics in education are and have been common to educators and educational theorists at least since Plato (e.g., see Chambliss, 1987) and are clearly manifested in such common and important distinctions made by educators as that between educa-tional product goals (what we want to achieve in the classroom or the school) and process goals (the restrictions that exist on how our prod-uct goals can be achieved) (see Teal & Reagan, 1973).

The third element of reflective thinking, the *narrative element*, is concerned with teachers' narratives. Teachers' accounts of their own experiences in the classroom take many forms and serve a variety of functions. Amy's journal is an example of one fairly common type of narrative. Other kinds of narrative discourse on the part of teachers are descriptions of critical events in the classroom, various types of logs and journals, conference reports completed jointly by teachers and supervisors or mentors, and self-interviewing. The key aspect of the narrative element of reflective thinking is that such narratives, whatever their form, serve to contextualize the classroom experience both for the teacher and for others and, by so doing, provide us with a much richer understanding of what takes place in the classroom and in the teacher's construction of reality than would otherwise be possible. Narrative accounts are becoming far more common today, especially in the preparation of teachers and in qualitative research on classroom practices (see Connelly & Clandinin, 1990; Goswami & Stillman, 1987; Zeichner & Liston, 1987), and they provide one of the most effective ways reflective practice can be encouraged.

A useful way of thinking about both the reflective teacher and the nature of the reflective practice in which the teacher will engage has been provided by Judith Irwin (1987):

> A reflective/analytic teacher is one who makes teaching decisions on the basis of a conscious awareness and careful consideration of (1) the assumptions on which the decisions are based and (2) the technical, educational, and ethical consequences of those decisions. These decisions are made before, during and after teaching actions. In order to make these decisions, the reflective/analytic teacher must have an extensive knowledge of the content to be taught, pedagogical and theoretical options, characteristics of individual students, and the situational constraints in the classroom, school and society in which they work. (p. 6)

Notice that this description includes virtually all the issues that have been discussed thus far. We see that the reflective teacher is first and foremost a decision maker who must make decisions consciously and rationally. Further, the reflective teacher must base his or her decisions and judgments on a solid body of content, including both technical and content knowledge, which are organized and reinterpreted according to the teacher's unique experiences. The reflective teacher must also demonstrate both ethical behavior and sensitivity, as well as sociocultural awareness. As Case et al. (1986) note:

The attendant characteristics of professions include conditions of practice that allow professionals to apply this knowledge freely to the practical affairs of their occupation and to use their knowledge, judgment, and skill within the structures of the ethical code of the profession. (p. 36)

Finally, it is important to note that reflective practice involves what the teacher does before entering the classroom (e.g., in terms of planning and preparation), while in the classroom (both while functioning as an educator and in all other roles expected of the classroom teacher), and retrospectively, after leaving the classroom. A good way of visualizing all this, as suggested earlier, is to think of a spiral, in which we begin with reflection-for-practice, move into reflection-in-practice, and then to reflection-on-practice—which inevitably leads us back to reflection-for-practice in an ongoing process.

Such a conceptualization of the reflective teacher makes clear how very much is being expected of the classroom teacher by advocates of reflective practice. Why, one might ask, should a teacher devote so much time and energy to becoming a reflective practitioner? What, in short, are the benefits of reflective practice? The benefits to be gained from reflective practice that have been suggested include the following:

- Reflective practice helps free teachers from impulsive, routine behavior
- Reflective practice allows teachers to act in a deliberate, intentional manner
- Reflective practice distinguishes teachers as educated human beings because it is one hallmark of intelligent action

Further, as we have already noted, reflective practice is useful in helping empower classroom teachers. Most important, though, reflective practice is a tool for individual teachers to improve their own teaching practice and to become better, more proficient, and more thoughtful professionals in their own right (see Zeichner & Liston, 1996).

BECOMING A REFLECTIVE PRACTITIONER

The process of becoming a reflective practitioner, like that of becoming a "good teacher," is a long and in many ways difficult one.

Becoming a reflective practitioner has much in common, in fact, with the process of becoming "Real" as the Skin Horse explained it to the Rabbit in the children's book *The Velveteen Rabbit* (Williams, 1981, pp. 14-16). Just as becoming Real takes time and happens after a toy has lost its hair and become shabby, so becoming a truly reflective teacher involves time, experience, and inevitably, a bit of wear around the edges. Every teacher, however, at every stage of his or her career can and should strive to become a reflective practitioner, knowing that only by making the effort to become reflective and analytic can one really be said to become a good teacher, just as every toy knows that being loved by a child is the only way to become Real.

Propositions for Reflection and Consideration

1. The study of reflective thinking need not result in an individual becoming a reflective practitioner. To become a reflective practitioner, a person must alter his or her behavior.
2. Reflective practitioners identify categories of knowledge that are requisite for successful reflective teaching (e.g., content, pedagogy, curriculum, learning, educational contexts, educational ends). They use these categories to analyze and modify practice.
3. Reflective practitioners are concerned with and involved in issues of social justice and ethics in education.
4. Reflective practitioners make conscious, rational decisions based on a solid and defensible knowledge base.

TOWARD A "CULTURE OF
INQUIRY" IN THE SCHOOL

*Disinterested and impartial inquiry is then far from
meaning that knowing is self-enclosed and irresponsible.
It means that there is no particular end set up in advance
so as to shut in the activities of observation, forming of
ideas, and application. Inquiry is emancipated. It is
encouraged to attend to every fact that is relevant to
defining the problem or need, and to follow up every
suggestion that promises a clue. The barriers to free
inquiry are so many and so solid that mankind is to be
congratulated that the very act of investigation is capable
of itself becoming a delightful and absorbing pursuit,
capable of enlisting on its side man's sporting instincts.*
John Dewey (1948, p. 146)

INQUIRY AS A COMPONENT OF GOOD
TEACHING: A CASE STUDY

Janet Rivers has been a sixth-grade teacher at Riverside Elementary School for 7 years. She is very popular with students, parents,
and colleagues and has a reputation for being an excellent, though
strict, teacher. Janet has always tried to follow the advice her cooperating teacher gave her when she student-taught: Never smile
until Christmas. For Janet, this means that she spends the first half of
the year ensuring that the students in her care know the classroom

28

rules and the behavior she expects from them, and she does this by posting the rules on a bulletin board in the front of her classroom, discussing each rule and the reasons behind the rule, and consistently enforcing the rules without exception. This approach has always worked for Janet in the past; only this year have problems arisen.

Chris Pappas is a bright, pleasant boy who had never had problems with any teacher before being placed in Janet's class. Both his parents have been involved in PTO activities and have been cooperative and supportive of the school. Chris has, according to the teachers who have had him in class in the past, been successful both academically and socially and has never had a significant conflict with a teacher. Almost from the very beginning of the current year, though, Chris and Janet have seemed to be on a collision course, which has been reflected in repeated and escalating confrontations. Chris has persisted in questioning and challenging the rules that Janet has tried to enforce, and dealing with him in class has become increasingly difficult for her.

At the first parent conference, Janet expressed her concerns about Chris's behavior to his parents, although she was also careful to assure them that his academic work did not appear to be affected. She was very surprised when Chris's mother told her that Chris spoke about her a great deal at home and felt very frustrated because he believed that she disliked him and that nothing he could do would please her. Chris's father then noted that, as far as he could tell, Chris's acting out in school was unique; his behavior at home had been fine, and neither his Sunday school teacher nor his Boy Scout leader had noted any similar problems.

At home that night, Janet could not get Chris out of her mind. She knew she had a serious problem with this youngster, one she had never had before, and she wanted to sort it out as soon as possible for everyone's sake. Chris's parents hadn't been at all hostile; indeed, at several points in the conference, his mother had seemed far more concerned about Janet's feelings than about Chris. She wasn't dealing with Chris effectively in class, and that, Janet decided, was the basic problem. Why was she having problems with Chris, when other teachers hadn't had similar problems? Regretfully, she realized that the only new variable in Chris's life seemed to be his teacher: Somehow, despite her best efforts, *she* must be at the root of the problem. What was she doing that was so different from what had come before in Chris's school experience? As she thought about her colleagues, Janet noted to herself that she tended to be far stricter than the other teachers at Riverside. She believed in discipline and in enforcing her rules fairly and evenhandedly and had never been one to display much emotion in class. Perhaps, though, a middle ground was possible. Janet decided to try an experiment in class the next day.

Janet had decided to try using active praise of Chris as a way of modifying his behavior; rather than focus on situations that had caused conflict in the past, she decided, just for this one day she would comment only on the positive things he did. If nothing else, she thought, perhaps this would be a step toward convincing Chris that she didn't dislike him. At one point, when the students were supposed to be sitting at their desks working, Janet noticed that Chris was standing next to Yasmin, quietly trying to explain a part of the worksheet that Yasmin clearly didn't understand. Biting her tongue to stop her rebuke, Janet instead said, "Chris, that's very helpful; I really appreciate you helping Yasmin. When you finish, though, would you sit back down and make sure you finish your own worksheet?" Chris looked up, a bit puzzled and perplexed, and Janet smiled at him. For the first time that year, Chris actually grinned back and said, "Yes ma'am," and quickly finished with Yasmin and sat down at his own desk. Janet was astounded because the situation had the makings of one of her standard arguments with Chris ("Chris, sit down!" "But I was just helping . . ." "Chris, I said sit down! You know the rules!").

Driving home that night, Janet mentally reviewed and reflected on what had taken place during the day. The class had gone very smoothly, with fewer hassles and problems than usual—in large part because she and Chris hadn't been constantly at each other, she had to admit. Chris had responded very well to her whenever she praised him, and a smile seemed to go a long way in getting his cooperation. She wondered whether perhaps her cooperating teacher could have been wrong, or at least whether the rule about not smiling until Christmas didn't work in Chris's case. She was still concerned about the implications of her experiment for her teaching methods generally. She still thought she couldn't treat students differently and still be fair, and yet she could not deny that a different approach seemed to work wonders for Chris. Janet decided to extend the experiment a bit longer and to discuss the issue of fairness and same treatment with her friend Emma Kopanski, a fourth-grade teacher at Riverside, at the first opportunity.

Analysis and Discussion. The case you just read is an interesting one for a variety of reasons. It raises questions about teaching methods, about ethics (especially the possible tension between effectiveness and fairness), and about reflection and its role in the classroom. Janet Rivers has been, by all accounts, a good teacher for several years. By the time she has Chris Pappas in her class, many of her classroom management behaviors have become habitual ones, which she is used to employing without thinking about or reflecting on them. Such habitual behaviors are natural and often useful: Each of us does many things every day without reflection or active thought. For instance, in driving a car, when I come to a red light, I do not take time to think about the meaning of the light or to make a thoughtful judgment to stop my car. Rather, I respond in a way that is essentially a conditioned response. Janet's habitual classroom behaviors, for which she has a theoretical rationale grounded in past experience, fails to achieve the desired results with Chris. Whatever one may think of Janet's philosophy of classroom management, at this point she begins acting in the way one would expect a good teacher to act. She is troubled and perplexed, and she subjects her habitual behavior to critical, reflective analysis.

In Janet's case, this reflective analysis results in the identification of the problem (her tried-and-true methods aren't working effectively in the case of Chris Pappas) and the formulation and implementation of an alternative strategy. Finally, as the strategy is implemented, Janet engages in an ongoing evaluation of its effectiveness. Notice that this case is concerned with the type of problem situation that might easily arise in virtually any classroom and, further, that Janet's response to the problem situation involves nothing more complex or sophisticated than common sense and a willingness to try new things. Nevertheless, Janet's behavior in this situation provides us with a good example of Dewey's notion of "free inquiry." Much classroom inquiry is of the informal sort illustrated in this case, but there is also considerable inquiry in classroom settings of a somewhat more formal sort. We turn now to several case studies in which different types of more formal inquiry are taking place in classroom settings.

INQUIRY AS RESEARCH:
FOUR CASE STUDIES

Albion Middle School is a large urban school with a culturally and linguistically diverse student body. Albion Middle School is of special interest to us because a variety of kinds of formal inquiry-based activities are taking place in the school. Let's look at several of these activities as examples of inquiry in the school context.

Reducing Mathematics Anxiety

A study of the effectiveness of an experimental mathematics anxiety reduction program is being conducted by Kim Sang, a graduate student from the local state university, in Duncan Andrew's eighth-grade beginning algebra classes. Kim provided Duncan with a set of prepackaged anxiety reduction activities for him to use in his third-period class; she is using his fifth-period class as a control group. The activities to be used with students include focused discussions about mathematics and fears of mathematics, role-playing activities in which mathematical knowledge must be applied to everyday problems (see Kogelman & Warren, 1978). The populations in the two classes were randomly assigned, and both contain roughly comparable populations. The study will use pre- and posttests to determine the effectiveness of the anxiety reduction activities. After the data have been collected, Kim will analyze them and write up the study for her thesis at the university; she hopes to publish a research article about the experiment. Duncan has been delighted to play a part in the research study because he has been bothered by the problems caused by mathematics anxiety among his students and hopes to learn how better to deal with the problems as a result of the study.

An Ethnographic Inquiry

A somewhat different kind of inquiry has been taking place in the English department, where Joan Richardson, a former teacher now enrolled in a doctoral program at a university in another state, is back and engaged in what she calls an "ethnographic" study. She has been sitting in on various ninth-grade English classes, taking notes and occasionally tape-recording classes. She has also been collecting class handouts and assignments and has spent a lot of time chatting with the English teachers about what they are trying to accomplish in their classes. She has also asked to read students' essays and plans to interview students both individually and in groups. She has even team-taught some classes with her former colleagues. Her goal, she says, is just to "understand what's happening in the English program," not to make recommendations or predictions. Although they've been a bit puzzled by what exactly she is trying to accomplish, Joan's former colleagues have enjoyed having her around again and appreciate the extra help she often provides in their classes. They've also noticed that she is very easy to talk with and a good person with whom they can talk over classroom problems.

Collaborative Research and the Science Curriculum

Irv Bowen, Jackie Lefevre, and Tanya O'Dell, three of the school's better science teachers, have been engaged in yet another type of inquiry. During the summer vacation, the three met several times to discuss ways they could improve their students' science learning. All three had been concerned that students at Albion were just memorizing content without gaining any real understanding of the scientific principles that undergirded the science curriculum. As a result of their summer meetings, they agreed to try modifying both the curriculum and their teaching methods in the seventh-grade general science classes that they all teach. During the current year, all three teachers have been trying to use more hands-on kinds of activities in their teaching and have stressed that students need to *discover* scientific concepts and ideas rather than simply "learn" them. For example, rather than simply lecture about the causes of volcanic eruptions, as he had done in the past, Irv divided his classes into teams of four or five students. Each team was given two liter-sized beakers and was told to fill one beaker with water and one with talcum powder. Irv then gave each team two straws and had a selected student in each team put the straws into the beakers and blow into the straws. He then had the class discuss what happened, and he explained the similarity to different sorts of volcanic eruptions.

The three teachers have continued to meet twice a month during the school year, on a Saturday at a local diner, to discuss the progress and problems that each has had, and all three have tried to keep a daily log of issues that have come up in their classes and the ways they've tried to deal with them. They have found that, by meeting outside the school setting, they feel freer to discuss problems and possible solutions and have agreed that nothing they share among themselves will be repeated at school. Some ideas they began with in September have been abandoned, others have been modified, and the year has turned out very differently from what they expected. In the case of the example given earlier, for instance, Irv decided afterward that, as a way of reducing the huge mess in his classroom, next year he would have a single team conduct the volcano experiment as a demonstration in front of the class. None of the three believe that they've "gotten it completely right" yet, and there have been some really tough times when everything seemed to go wrong, but on the whole their experience has been a positive one. None of the three teachers have any intention of publishing the results of their activities, nor are any using the experience for advanced degrees. They see themselves simply as teachers trying to improve their practice in a collaborative, supportive way.

Involving Students in Inquiry

Bill Jackson has been teaching social studies at Albion since it opened 15 years ago. One of only a small number of African American teachers in the district, Bill is widely acknowledged as an outstanding teacher whose enthusiasm for his subject is contagious for even the most "difficult" students. This year has been no exception. There has been a controversial debate in the county about the possible placement of a low-level nuclear waste facility near the town, and Bill and his eighth-grade students have spent most of the year talking and arguing about and researching the debate. They have worked as a team, with Bill functioning mainly as a group facilitator, to find out as much as they could not only about the nature and risks posed by such a facility but also about the policy-making process and how they could make their own concerns heard. His students have spent a great deal of time in both the school and the local public library and have attended several town council meetings, as well as meetings of the local zoning board. Bill and his students even toured a nearby power station after the manager saw them at a zoning board meeting and invited them to see the plant in person. Bill readily admits that he knew almost nothing about nuclear power and nuclear waste facilities before the year started and says that he and his students have really worked together to learn what they needed to know.

Analysis and Discussion. These four case studies are concerned with the process of inquiry in a school context, but the nature and purposes of the inquiries, as well as the ways they are conducted and how one would evaluate them, are very different in many ways. In the first case study, we are presented with a fairly traditional research study that has identifiable dependent and independent variables and an experimental group and a control group. The researcher in this study is seeking to be neutral and objective, and the subjects of the study are observed in terms of behavioral changes that occur as a result of planned activities designed to modify behavior. The second case is also a university-driven study, but the researcher is immersed in what she is studying, and is, in fact, a participant in her own study. Further, whereas in the first study the researcher was presumably concerned with the generalizability of her results (with the study's external validity), in the second study Joan is interested only in "understanding"—rejecting, it would seem, any concern with generalizability. The third case study presented a very different kind of inquiry; indeed, many people would say that only the first two cases, or perhaps even only the first, are really examples of educational research. What Irv Bowen, Jackie Lefevre, and Tanya O'Dell are engaging in is certainly different from the first two cases, and yet they, too, are trying to study their classes, engage in reflective problem solving, develop hypotheses, test their hypotheses, and so on. What's more, they are doing so *together,* both challenging and supporting one another as they come to understand and, they hope, improve their teaching practice. Even more than in Joan Richardson's case, they are participants in their own study; in fact, in a way one could say that they and their behaviors in the classroom are one focus for their inquiry. The kind of inquiry in which these three science teachers are engaging is sometimes called the *teacher as researcher* model or approach. Last, in the fourth case study we see a teacher, Bill Jackson, and his students working together on an issue of common concern. In this last case, the collaboration that characterized the three science teachers engaging in the process of teacher as researcher is taking place, not among teachers, but between the teacher and his students. In short, the "subjects" have themselves become the "researchers," and they are not only engaged in inquiry but are themselves determining the nature, purposes, and direction of that inquiry.

As indicated earlier, many people would argue that not all the cases discussed are really examples of research. The important point, for our purposes here, is not whether these cases are all instances of research, although we believe that they are. Rather, the significant issue here is that all four cases demonstrate individuals trying to understand, in a more or less formal manner, some aspect of their world. Although these four cases do differ in some very important ways, they also share common features, and it is to a discussion of these shared features of the process of inquiry that we now turn.

THE CONCEPT OF INQUIRY

Yvonna Lincoln and Egon Guba, two well-known and highly respected qualitative researchers, begin their book *Naturalistic Inquiry* (1985) by commenting:

> The history of humankind is replete with instances of attempts to understand the world. Our curiosity has been directed at the same fundamental questions throughout time; our progress as inquirers can be charted by noting the various efforts made to deal with those questions. What is the world? How can we come to know it? How can we control it for our purposes? What is, after all, the *truth* about these matters? (p. 14)

This quote provides an excellent starting point for making sense of the concept of inquiry. Basically, as the quote suggests, *inquiry* refers to our attempts to understand and make sense of the world (or parts of the world) around us. Inquiry can be more or less formal, more or less rigorous, and can involve a wide range of techniques, methods, and procedures, as well as produce very different kinds of outcomes or final products. The process of inquiry can even entail very different (and sometimes incompatible) ideas and assumptions about the nature of knowledge and knowing, and different individuals will often approach the process of inquiry in quite different ways. Further, as Lincoln and Guba argue, inquiry is ultimately concerned with some common fundamental issues. In education, for instance, virtually all research and inquiry is ultimately concerned with the improvement of teaching and learning. This having been said, of course, it is also important to note that the focus of any specific inquiry will be far narrower and will be concerned with only a small part of this broader and more general issue. For example, we find inquiries concerned with organizational matters, ethical matters, pedagogical matters, curricular matters, and so on, all of which constitutes perfectly appropriate educational inquiry. As all of this would suggest, no single model of inquiry includes all cases and types of educational inquiry. Rather, many different models have been suggested to describe the inquiry process, and we now briefly examine a few of these models.

Perhaps the most common conceptualization of the inquiry process is what is somewhat misleadingly called the *scientific method*. This is a formalized description of the process in which scientists (and especially those working in the physical sciences) are presumed to engage as they try to discover new knowledge. The scientific method can be broken down into five distinct steps: (a) identification of a problem, (b) definition of the problem, (c) formulation of hypotheses, (d) projection of consequences, and (e) testing of hypotheses (see, e.g., Fraenkel & Wallen, 1990, pp. 6-7). The goal of using the scientific method is to test ideas about the world in a formal, public, and rigorous manner. Researchers who try to use the scientific method are attempting to ensure the neutrality and objectivity of their research and the results of their research; an underlying theme of the scientific method is that the researcher or inquirer should be irrelevant to the research or inquiry being conducted. Such a view exemplifies what is known as the *positivist* (or sometimes *postpositivist*) paradigm of educational research.

Use of the scientific method in conducting educational research is often appropriate and valuable. Much of what is known about aspects of good teaching and of student learning comes from research conducted in this way. The study being conducted at Albion Middle School on mathematics anxiety reduction by Kim Sang is an example of inquiry grounded in the scientific method. Research of this kind has some important limitations, however. Because of its underlying assumptions, research based on the scientific method excludes certain in-depth sorts of studies and inquiries and inevitably undervalues or rejects altogether the role of intuition in inquiry. In contrasting different approaches to educational inquiry, it is useful to consider a distinction suggested by the anthropologist Clifford Geertz, who distinguishes between two kinds of research: (a) that which provides us with a *thin description* of a context and (b) that which gives us a *thick description* (Geertz, 1973, 1983). To obtain a thick description, the researcher or inquirer must be immersed in the context of the inquiry; indeed, it is often best if the researcher is actually a participant in the study (see Hammersley, 1990, 1992; Spradley, 1980; Whyte, 1991). The scientific method approach to inquiry can provide us with detailed information about the reading achievement of children in a third-grade class and can point out variables that correlate with increased achievement. An ethnographic study, however, could tell us a great deal more about the way the children and the teacher interact in that same third-grade class, as well as help us understand how both the teacher and the children make sense of the classroom (how each constructs her or his reality). The former type of inquiry would provide us with a thin description, the latter with a thick description. Both can be very useful in improving education; neither on its own gives us a complete picture.

The American philosopher of education John Dewey wrote extensively about the application of the scientific method to social and educational problems. Dewey, however, conceived of the scientific method in a somewhat broader way than that discussed earlier (see Sherman & Webb, 1988, pp. 11-18). Rather than see inquiry as an activity set apart from normal, everyday life, Dewey believed that "inquiry is the life-blood of every science and is constantly engaged in every art, craft and profession" (Dewey, 1938, p. 4). Further, he recognized that "inquiry is a mode of activity that is socially conditioned and that has cultural consequences" (p. 19) and that when we are engaged in the process of inquiry,

> in actual experience, there is never any . . . isolated singular object or event; *an* object or event is always a special part, phase, or aspect, of an environing experienced world—a situation. The singular object stands out conspicuously because of its especial focal and crucial position at a given time in determination of some problem of use or enjoyment which the *total* complex environment presents. There is always a *field* in which observation of *this* or *that* object or event occurs. (p. 67)

In short, the approach to inquiry suggested by Dewey attempts to place inquiry and its objects in a social and normative context. In a discussion of Dewey's views on the process of inquiry, Henry Levin (1991) explains:

> The inquiry approach is a systematic and disciplined method for understanding problems, finding and implementing solutions, and assessing their results. It is a process for incorporating values, obtaining information on alternatives, and building on the strengths and talents of staff, parents, and students. It is also an approach to testing solutions to see if they work. (p. 2)

The idea that it is necessary for us to contextualize our inquiry and to view inquiry as a dynamic rather than as a static process has provided the foundation for what is commonly known as *qualitative* or *naturalistic* inquiry (see Denzin & Lincoln, 1994; Erlandson, Harris, Skipper, & Allen, 1993). Studies that are qualitative or naturalistic in orientation are concerned with providing a thick description of a context (to use Geertz's terminology) and attempt to offer a holistic perspective of the social and cultural context in which they occur. An important facet of such inquiries is that they presuppose the existence of multiple, constructed realities, rather than a single, objective reality. Thus, the point of Joan Richardson's study is, in essence, to understand how teachers in the English program make sense of their world and how students in their classes make sense of the same classroom situations. To some extent, each individual in each classroom is engaged in constructing her or his own reality, and the goal of the researcher is to try to understand all these different constructions of reality.

As the inquirer begins a naturalistic study, she or he necessarily becomes part of what is being studied. The researcher in a classroom is not invisible to the teacher and students, and her or his presence in the room (no matter how unobtrusive the person attempts to be) does change the setting of the study. As a result, some researchers seek to make the best of this situation by becoming active participants in their own studies, as Joan Richardson did to a limited extent. When this takes place, we speak of *participant observation* types of research (Spradley, 1980). Further, on some occasions, the inquiry is actually being conducted by the participants themselves for their own ends, as is the case with both the three science teachers and Bill Jackson.

Inquiry of this sort is called *action research* because its primary objective is to improve practice (see Bissex & Bullock, 1987; Kemmis & McTaggart, 1988; Mohr & MacLean, 1987; Norlander et al., 1997, pp. 44-46). We are concerned at this point, though, not so much with the different types of inquiry; rather, our concern is with the characteristics necessary for an individual to engage in inquiry.

In all four examples of inquiry taking place at Albion Middle School, the individuals involved share some characteristics that are central to the inquiry process. These individual characteristics are (a) intellectual curiosity, (b) motivation, (c) openness in inquiry, and (d) openness to challenge. Each of these characteristics is discussed briefly next.

All inquiry is ultimately based on curiosity. Dewey (1933, pp. 36-39) suggests three developmental stages of curiosity: (a) *organic* (or *physiological*) *curiosity*, of the sort one sees in a cat playing with a ball of string or in a toddler "getting into everything"; (b) *social curiosity*, in which facts are sought from others (the "why?" stage of child development); and (c) *intellectual curiosity*, which is characterized, in Dewey's words, by the transformation of curiosity "into interest in finding out for oneself the answers to questions that are aroused by contact with persons and things" (p. 39). It is with the development and nurturing of intellectual curiosity that the schools should be concerned for both students and teachers. All too often, however, we find that the schooling experience has just the opposite effect and is thus actually inimical to the emergence of inquiry. As Dewey comments,

> Bacon's saying that we must become as little children in order to enter the kingdom of science is at once a reminder of the open-minded and flexible wonder of childhood and of the ease with which this endowment is lost. Some lose it in indifference or carelessness; others in a frivolous flippancy; many escape these evils only to become incased in a hard dogmatism that is equally fatal to this spirit of wonder. (p. 39)

Indeed, this "spirit of wonder" undergirds intellectual curiosity, and its loss obviously affects all types of learning and inquiry. As Thomas Green (1971) has argued, "One way to destroy the motivation to learn is to effectively abort the childlike capacity for awe and wonder" (p. 201).

Closely related to intellectual curiosity as a condition for individual inquiry is motivation. Just as educators concern themselves with motivating students in the classroom, so too must we consider the need for personal motivation in building on and responding to intellectual curiosity. Central to the idea of motivation in this regard is the need for the object of our inquiry to constitute, in Dewey's words, a "real" problem. As Dewey (1916/1944) has noted:

> It is indispensable to discriminate between a genuine and simulated or mock problems. . . Is the experience a personal thing of such a nature as inherently to stimulate and direct observation of the connections involved, and to lead to inference and its testing? Or is it imposed from without? (p. 155)

If the object or purpose of the inquiry is really a legitimate problem, in short, then the need for motivation is met; otherwise, the inquiry is simply an external (and, essentially, a nonreflective) activity that will have little benefit to the individual involved.

For true inquiry to take place, it is essential that the individual be open to differing—and even unexpected and surprising—evidence and interpretations. The teachers in every one of the five case studies presented demonstrated such openness to the process of inquiry, although, to be sure, they pursued their inquiries in very different ways. An important element of this openness to the process of inquiry is the recognition that, in any inquiry, the evidence (e.g., factual data, observations) does not "speak for itself"; rather, in every instance, the observer/inquirer must make sense of the evidence by placing it in a conceptual and theoretical context. As the philosopher of science Paul Feyerabend (1978) has explained, "On closer analysis we even find that science knows no 'bare facts' at all but that the 'facts' that enter our knowledge are already viewed in a certain way and are, therefore, essentially ideational" (p. 19). In other words, to a certain extent any organization or framework that we impose on reality is just that—an imposition that we employ to help us understand and make sense of reality, rather than an actual picture of reality. This means that we must strive to consider and reflect on not only the evidence that would appear to support our own construction of reality but also (perhaps especially) evidence that does *not* fit our expectations.

Finally, an important aspect of inquiry is that we must remain open to challenge and criticism. Inquiry is best understood as a social and public endeavor and is often most effectively undertaken in a communal context. This does not necessarily mean that the actual inquiry undertaken must be a group activity, but it does mean that the process, as well as the results of the inquiry, must be subject to the scrutiny and evaluation of others. This scrutiny and evaluation can take place in many different ways: the defense of a university thesis or dissertation, the submission of the results of an inquiry to a scholarly journal, the presentation of an inquiry at a public or professional meeting, the discussion of the inquiry in informal settings with colleagues. Although it is true that none of us much like or enjoy being told or shown that we are wrong or in error or that we have overlooked an important aspect of a context we are studying, such corrections are essential if our inquiries are to be credible ones.

A CULTURE OF
INQUIRY IN THE SCHOOL

Thus far, we have discussed the concept of inquiry and indicated some general attributes that would characterize the individual teacher as she or he engages in inquiry. At this point, we need to turn our focus from the individual to the school community and to describe what a school in which a culture of inquiry has been developed would look like. It is important to remember that, in any school, some inquiry will be taking place. Individual teachers, in their daily lives, very often engage in informal types of inquiry as part of their normal classroom activities (see Norlander-Case et al., 1998). This chapter, for instance, began with the case of Janet Rivers, who was clearly engaged in inquiry, although of an informal sort. Often, too, individual teachers will seek to engage in more formal types of inquiry. Although all of this is to the good, it does not on its own mean that the school in which these teachers work models a culture of inquiry, any more than a school in which some teachers are bilingual would automatically be a bilingual school. Rather, a school in which a culture of inquiry exists is a school in which there is a broad, fairly general consensus about the desirability of and need for inquiry as part of the educational process. In such a school, teachers, administrators, and students, as well as university faculty where possible, will all, to varying degrees, participate in the identification and exploration of topics of inquiry. As the authors of the Holmes Group report *Tomorrow's Schools* (1990) comment:

> Inquiry in the Professional Development School should be a way for teachers, administrators, and professors to come together on equal footing. It should help forge a shared professional identity in schools and universities. And it should serve as a professional norm around which collaboration can take place, bringing together the many parties who are concerned for improving schools. (p. 60)

A culture of inquiry, in short, entails not merely teachers engaged in inquiry but teachers and others collaboratively and collegially seeking to understand better and thus improve aspects of the schooling experience. For a culture of inquiry to exist and be maintained in a school, an ongoing commitment to valuing curiosity, mutual respect and support among teachers and between teachers and administrators, a willingness to try new ideas and practices, and the ability to remain open to the unforeseen and unexpected are required. Further, an important element of such a school will be the nature of the leadership present, as we discuss in detail in Chapter 6. In the Gilbert and Sullivan operetta *The Gondoliers*, the Duke of Plaza-Toro is humorously described as "leading his regiment from behind." Without dwelling on the point here, let's just note that it is simply not possible to have a school in which a culture of inquiry exists led by an administrator who exemplifies what might be termed the "Duke of Plaza-Toro" style of leadership. The school in which a culture of inquiry exists will, then, be a very unusual kind of institution and will in many ways operate quite differently from most schools today. It will, in short, be a school in which inquiry plays a key role in the development and process of reflective, analytic practice.

THE TEACHER AS RESEARCHER

An important component of a school in which a culture of inquiry exists is that teachers will see themselves, and will be seen by others, as engaging in ongoing inquiry-based activities. Such involvement in research on the part of teachers is arguably a key part of the development of reflective, analytic practice on the part of the classroom teacher. As Bogdan and Biklen (1992) have explained, "Because teachers acting as researchers not only perform their duties but also watch themselves, they step back and, distanced from immediate conflicts, they are able to gain a larger view of what is happening" (p. 218). At this point, we turn to several case studies in which we can see teachers functioning as teacher-researchers.

Phonics or Whole Language?

Sara Bidwell is an experienced second-grade teacher in a small elementary school in Sweetmore, a semirural area. She is the only second-grade teacher in the school and, therefore, has a wide range of ability levels represented in her classroom. In recent years, Sara has also had several children with learning disabilities mainstreamed in her classroom for large portions of the day. This year, Sara's class has 20 children; the range of abilities is the greatest she has experienced thus far in her career.

One of the most important parts of her job, Sara believes, is the teaching of reading. Over the years, Sara has relied on phonics and the use of basal readers as her primary method of instruction in teaching children to read. She has been very successful each year with about half of the children in her classes, with many of them achieving at and even above grade level. At the same time, however, Sara has noticed that many other children in her classes have been considerably less successful in learning to read. In particular, she is concerned that the children are not doing as well on comprehension as she believes they can. In her early years of teaching, Sara believed that children who were having problems learning to read were themselves to blame. Very often, these children had other problems in school as well, and Sara had thought that perhaps they were just not as bright or as motivated as their more successful classmates.

During the past few years, however, Sara has changed her mind, as she has become less critical of the children and more critical of her own teaching. She has become especially concerned with the basal readers she was once quite happy with; now, she sees them as too restrictive and boring for the children she is trying to teach. Although Sara has been ready for a change of some sort for several years, she hasn't felt comfortable or sure enough to try any radical changes. Instead, she has been gradually trying to use more trade books in her teaching and has gone out of her way to find stories and poems she thinks her second graders will find interesting.

During the summer, the Sweetmore Board of Education, whose membership has almost completely changed as a result of the last two town elections, hired both a new superintendent and a new principal for the elementary school. For the first time in Sweetmore's history, both of these administrators are women, and both have been hired by the board of education with an explicit mandate for change. The principal of the elementary school has made it clear that one of her major goals for the current school year is to encourage teachers to vary curricula and instructional methods to suit individual student needs, interests, and learning styles. To support such changes, some funding has been made available for workshops, in-service training, university courses, curricular materials, and technical assistance. This is a significant departure from past practice in Sweetmore, and many teachers remain skeptical about whether the administration and school board are really serious about these changes. Sara, however, has been very excited about these efforts from the very beginning and has decided to seize the opportunity to address some of her concerns about teaching reading.

On the basis of several articles she has read in her teacher magazines, Sara has decided to learn all she can about the *whole language philosophy*. With the assistance of the new principal, she has written a professional development plan for the school year. The plan requires that she take a course at the local university that will deal with whole language. She also plans to do additional professional reading in her spare time and to attend a workshop at the state reading association conference, with sessions on both whole language and "Reading Recovery." A key part of Sara's professional development plan is that she will, on the basis of her classroom applications of what she learns, conduct some type of research study to be completed by the end of June. Sara has already been to the university library and has selected recent books concerned with whole language and the teaching of reading.

On the advice of a friend who recently graduated from a teacher preparation program, Sara has decided to keep a journal to document what takes place during the year. Her journal consists of two parts: (a) The left side of each page is used for recording ideas and information she gets from her reading, her university course, in-service sessions, conversations she has with her colleagues, and so on; and (b) the right side of each page is used for recording comments to herself about the ideas and information she is gaining. The left side of the journal Sara initially thought would be the most useful, but she has since decided that the comments on the right side, where she is actually reflecting, conducting ongoing dialogue with herself, trying to make sense of all she is learning, and attempting to figure out how to apply this to her classroom is the more valuable part of the journal.

At this point, Sara does not yet know exactly how she will implement the whole language philosophy in her classroom, and so her plans for conducting some sort of research remain vague. She is undecided about whether she can, or should, try to use some kind of experimental design in her research and is aware that because she has only one class, this could be difficult (see Jaeger, 1988; Kerlinger, 1973). She is quite sure that some of the more important information about what works in her classroom will probably come from systematic observations of individual children, but she is unsure how to make such observations. The principal has suggested trying to get students from the local university to assist her with these observations, but Sara is not sure whom to contact. She also knows that she wants to introduce student portfolios and portfolio assessment in her class. If she goes ahead with this, she should be able to collect quite a bit of documentary evidence about changes taking place with individual children. Although she isn't certain how to do it, Sara also thinks she probably ought to include some kind of pre- and posttest information if she wants to convince other teachers and parents, as well as other members of the community, that the changes have really had beneficial outcomes, thereby influencing subsequent policy decisions.

As she thinks about what she is trying to accomplish and how different this school year has been from her earlier experiences, Sara is exhausted and a bit overwhelmed. She is also excited, though, and this feeling makes her think she just may be on to something.

Understanding the Dropout Problem

Center Park High School is a large inner-city school with an enrollment of approximately 1,800 students. The majority of students at Center Park High School come from single-parent families, and the rate of unemployment and underemployment in the area is among the highest in the city. The crime rate has been rising dramatically in recent years, and school violence has also been increasing. Demographically, the student body is roughly 60% Hispanic, 30% African American, 5% Asian, and 5% white. The staff at Center Park High School includes several Hispanic and African American teachers but nevertheless remains overwhelmingly white.

Center Park High School is fortunate in that many of its teachers and administrators are experienced, skilled, effective, and committed to the students. Nonetheless, despite the staff's best efforts, nearly half of the 9th-grade class will drop out before 10th grade each year. This has been an ongoing problem at Center Park High School, and in the last few years the 9th-grade teaching staff have become more vocal about their frustrations and concerns with the situation. This year, a core group of 9th-grade teachers have decided to work together to try to address this problem.

The teachers began by deciding that a big part of the problem may be their lack of information about their students and the lives their students lead. They agreed that they had a limited amount of factual knowledge about their students and that although this knowledge, together with their intuition (informed as it was by their experience and concern), was useful, it was also incomplete. After reading and discussing Michelle Fine's book *Framing Dropouts* (1991), which the principal had suggested to one of the teachers, the teachers decided that the best way for them to start to address the dropout problem was by outlining the assumptions they have been making about their students; they agreed on the following list:

- Many parents do not care about their children's achievement in school.
- Many students have no place to study.
- Many students who are at risk for dropping out work long hours after school and at night to help their families financially.
- Some students come to school, not for any academic or vocational reason, but rather to socialize with other students.
- Some students at risk for dropping out are already involved in the drug culture.
- Some students at risk for dropping out understand and speak very little English.
- Many students at risk for dropping out appear to have learned very little in elementary and middle school.

After compiling this list, the teachers formed four task groups to try to determine the extent to which their assumptions were well founded. The first task group was assigned the job of examining the cumulative records of all ninth graders from the previous year in the hope of finding patterns that would help in predicting which types of students are most likely to drop out of school. Particular attention was to be paid to attendance records, grades, test scores, and teacher comments about behavior and achievement. The second task group was to try to locate students from the previous year's ninth grade who had dropped out and to interview them about why they decided to leave school. The third task group was to try to duplicate the efforts of the second task group but, instead of dropouts, was to interview students who are now 10th graders at Center Park High School to try to understand why they stayed in school. The fourth task group was assigned the job of interviewing parents of both dropouts and those students who continued on at Center Park High School to determine possible effects of parental and extraschool contributions to this decision.

When the core group of ninth-grade teachers met together in January to share their findings, they were surprised to discover how much more complex and complicated the situation was than they had expected. They found that many of their assumptions had proved to be true for particular students but not, as a general rule, to anywhere near the extent they had anticipated. For instance, they found that although a few parents were uninterested in the school and their children's success or failure at school, most cared deeply about their children's successes and problems at school. They also found, much to their surprise, that for many parents the school was a hostile, alien environment and that feelings of disempowerment on the part of parents were common when faced with school problems.

A common theme among both students who had dropped out and students who had remained in school was that the need for employment played a central role in their lives and that, as a result of their work roles, they often had no spare time in which to study. Further, they frequently came to school too tired to pay much attention to what was taking place in class.

Many students who had dropped out of school reported that they had been able to coast through their earlier schooling and that they had suddenly realized they did not have the background knowledge to even begin the ninth-grade curriculum. They also appeared generally to lack even fairly basic study skills that should have been learned earlier in their school experiences. As a consequence, they had not understood what was taking place in the classroom, felt stupid when comparing themselves with their more successful classmates, and could not remember enough of the material presented in class to pass the tests. So that others would not see them as less intelligent, these students commonly chose to drop out rather than admit their problems.

The core group of teachers were especially surprised when they discussed drug use among those who had dropped out. Although those who had dropped out did have a much higher rate of drug abuse than those who had remained in school, in many cases this seemed to have been a consequence of having dropped out rather than the other way around.

The task group that examined students' cumulative records provided some interesting information as well. The records indicated, as expected, a strong correlation between high absenteeism and subject matter failures. The task group also found, in their study of teacher comments, that in some cases a single student might be described in very different ways by different teachers. This had led the group to examine teacher grades, and they found that some teachers (including several who had reputations as "good" teachers) had had, year after year, very high rates of student failures. Because these teachers were spread throughout the school, teaching different subjects, if an at-risk student were unlucky enough to find her- or himself in classes with several of these "hard graders," the student was almost certain to fail.

Finally, in talking with both dropouts and students who had continued at Center Park High School, the teachers discovered two consistent and powerful themes. First, all students they talked with had little sense of belonging. Even though there were teachers who cared, the constant changing of subjects and teachers left little time for sustained assistance or interaction. Second, much of the curriculum was, from the students' perspective, boring and inactive, and far too much instruction consisted solely of lecture. One interviewed student commented in passing that learning was "when you copy down in your notebook what the teacher says."

By the end of their meeting, the core group of ninth-grade teachers thought they had a much better, albeit in many ways more complicated, view of how students viewed school. Now, they thought they were ready to move on and try to change things.

Using Computers to Teach Writing

Paul Roper is in his fifth year of teaching English at Dr. Martin Luther King, Jr., Middle School, a magnet school for mathematics, science, and technology in a medium-sized city. Students at King Middle School are representative of the city's population and include students from diverse ethnic and economic backgrounds, as well as students with a wide range of aptitudes, interests, and abilities.

Paul has found a common denominator in this diversity, however. Most of his students are poor writers. The more successful students in his classes are able to produce technically correct writing, but it is almost always forced. Many of his students, though, cannot even prepare a decent one-page essay. This has been very disturbing to Paul, who has always had his students write a great deal. Because he believes writing to be very important both academically and socially, Paul has tried to return the corrected papers to his students within a day—a practice that he definitely believes is effective but that has also used up much of his "nonschool" time. As a result of his efforts, Paul has been a more successful writing teacher than many of his colleagues, but he is far from satisfied with his performance because he believes that far more could be done.

Recently, Paul has stopped using textbooks altogether and instead has been using a variety of short stories, novels, essays, and poems. This new approach seems to have created greater student interest and has led to far more lively discussions in class, but Paul has not yet noticed any significant improvement in his students' writing. Although he is not comfortable with the technology, Paul has begun to think about using the school's computer lab as a way of encouraging students to write. He has noticed that Steve Major, a special education teacher at King Middle School, seems to have had remarkable success using the lab; some of his students, who had never written much of anything before, are now writing three or four pages. In addition, the students' interactions with the computer seem to have made them more willing to rewrite their papers, as well as more animated and willing to share and discuss their work with others. Steve believes that his students have really "found their voice" for the first time, writing about personal issues in their lives, and has strongly recommended that Paul give the computer lab a try.

Paul is interested in trying the lab but would like to do so in an experimental way. He has two classes of seventh graders that are quite similar and with roughly comparable levels of writing ability. His goal is to use the lab with one group and his other methods with the other class and then to compare the results. He is very unsure, though, of what exactly to do and is afraid that his inexperience in both using the computer lab and conducting research will prevent him from accomplishing anything worthwhile. Paul begins to think about the different ways he could organize the instruction for each class and then assess the difference in outcomes. He wonders how many factors he should keep the same and how many he could change at one time and still be able to determine what made a difference and what didn't. Could he use an experimental or quasi-experimental design? Should he use pre- and posttests to assess gains, and, if so, what tests would fit with the curriculum? Research methods of this type would give strength to his conclusions no matter what the outcome might be. But would he really gain deeper understanding and insights into what had taken place?

Analysis and Discussion. These three case studies provide us with a very different kinds of school-based research scenarios. Each case presents us with a different type of research problem and a different context in which the problem is to be addressed. Further, two cases (Sara Bidwell's concern with teaching reading and Paul Roper's concern with teaching writing) involve primarily one teacher, whereas the third case (Center Park High School and its dropout problem) is a collaborative effort involving several teachers. All three of these cases, however, exemplify the concern raised earlier in this chapter about the need for developing a culture of inquiry in the school, and all three cases are ultimately concerned with what might be called *action research* in the school setting (see Bissex & Bullock, 1987; Goswami & Stillman, 1987; Kemmis & McTaggart, 1988).

The three cases are similar in another important way as well. In all three cases, the research problem is the result of a concern or question raised by teachers on the basis of their own observations and experiences in the classroom and school context; that is, the research questions these teachers are trying to address arise from their own curiosity and worries, and not as a result of a literature search of some sort. This is an important point because it is one of the ways in which action research tends to differ from more traditional kinds of educational research. In other words, in all three of these case studies, we see examples of what might be called *teacher-driven research*.

These three case studies are also useful for us because they provide an array of possibilities with respect to appropriate research methodologies. One lesson that should be clear from these cases is that no single method of research could answer all the different questions that have been raised; indeed, what these three cases would lead us to believe is that there is no single model of inquiry and that research is best viewed as a dynamic, rather than a static, process that seeks to take into account the incredible complexity of human beings and human social settings (e.g., classrooms). The task of the professional educator must be to examine the research question that she or he faces and to determine which of the myriad research methodologies will be best suited to providing the kind of information she or he wants to acquire. There is no more a "correct" approach to research than there is a "correct" way of teaching a child to read; a different approach and methodology must be used in each case, and the determination of which approach and method should be tried in any particular context is the responsibility of the teacher as an educational professional. At this point, let's examine each of the three case studies and try to identify the kinds of research methodologies that might be best suited and most appropriate in each case.

In the case of Sara Bidwell, we have a classroom teacher who has been monitoring what works and what doesn't work in her own classroom as she tries to teach children to read. For Sara, the impetus for inquiry is not an abstract curiosity, nor is it a puzzle that has emerged in the professional literature. Rather, it is the kind of concern that almost all classroom teachers face as a result of their daily classroom practice. Sara has begun with her problem—how to do a better job teaching children in her class to read—and has committed herself to learning more about alternative approaches to the teaching of reading with which she is not yet really familiar. She has, in short, already made an effort to link the topic and focus of her personal inquiry to the existing professional knowledge base. Further, Sara has taken the crucial step of deciding, at least in tentative form, how to go about addressing her inquiry. By using a split-page journal, Sara has ensured that she will be able to track her own growing database, as well as her own understanding of that database. In essence, keeping a reflective journal provides us with a simple and integrated method of combining conversations, observations, insights, and so on as we construct our understanding of what is taking place. The journal format also allows us the luxury of backtracking and watching our own process of discovery and understanding. Through such systematic means, teachers can review and challenge their own thinking, understandings, and practice and ultimately can help contribute to the knowledge base in their own profession. This is one way truly dedicated professionals can be distinguished from other workers.

Sara's process of inquiry hinges on the changes that she will be implementing in her classroom, and it is not possible for her to decide what sort of study she wishes to conduct until she has decided what exactly she is to do in terms of implementing the whole language philosophy in her classroom and what her goals for these changes are. Once she has come up with a plan for implementing the change in her teaching, she could employ any of a wide array of research methods. She has already decided that she would like to include in her study some sort of pre- and posttest, presumably of reading ability, comprehension, and so forth. Such pre- and posttesting can be combined with other types of research activities as well, including individual case studies of children, and comparisons of the reading achievement of Sara's children with comparable children receiving a more traditional kind of instruction. It would also be possible for Sara to focus her study, not so much on improvement in children's learning, but on changes in children's attitudes about reading. Obviously, one would go about studying such attitudinal changes in a somewhat different manner than one would use if improvements in reading comprehension, for example, were the focus of the research. In short, Sara's experience makes clear that it is important to decide what kinds of things one wants to know before one can adopt and implement specific research strategies.

In the case of Center Park High School, we are presented with a case of collaborative research being undertaken by a group of ninth-grade teachers who share a concern about the problem of the ninth-grade dropout rate at their school. Again, as was the case with Sara Bidwell, these teachers have identified a problem in their own experience to study. Although the problem they are trying to address is a common one in urban schools and has received extensive discussion in the professional literature, the teachers themselves are interested in the problem primarily because it affects them and their students. Although no mention is made in this case of anyone keeping a journal, the teachers together engage in a process that is very similar in purpose to at least some aspects of a reflective journal. Specifically, the teachers begin by making a list of things they believe to be true that relate to the high dropout rate. In essence, this means they are engaging in both individual and group reflection. Once they have completed their list of assumptions, they then use that list as the basis for their inquiry. On the basis of the beliefs they identified as their starting assumptions (their *hypotheses*, to use research jargon), they sort themselves into four task groups and try to determine the extent to which each of their assumptions is valid. Each of the task groups makes use of a somewhat different strategy, determined in large part by the kind of information they are seeking. For instance, the first task group, which focused on the analysis of students' cumulative records, would have used basic statistical procedures to identify correlations among such variables as attendance, grades, test scores, teacher comments, and the likelihood of an individual student dropping out of school. The other three task groups all used interviewing techniques. This combination of quantitative and qualitative research methods helps ensure that the information the teachers gather will provide as complete a picture as possible of what is taking place. An important aspect of the Center Park High School collaborative study is that the teachers remained open to surprises; they were willing to see their starting assumptions proved wrong, or at least misleading. This openness to being wrong is arguably the most important element not only of any sort of research activity but also of reflection and reflective practice. Finally, it is worth noting that the only outcome of the Center Park High School study thus far is a greater understanding of what is taking place on the part of the teachers; the next step, which is not detailed in our case study, is for the teachers to attempt to fashion a response to their new understanding of the problem.

Paul Roper presents an interesting case because he exemplifies the Deweyan notion of problem solving that we have already discussed (see Dewey, 1910, 1933, 1938). He is puzzled by his students' lack of writing skills and is intrigued by the potential he believes may exist in the use of computers. His approach is basically an open-minded one; it isn't at all clear that he is sure the use of computers with his students will be as successful as it has been for Steve Major, but he is willing to try. He is deliberating seeking a research methodology that will allow him to compare two comparable groups and knows that his own inexperience in using computers may be a factor. In short, he has already decided, in a tentative fashion, on the appropriate research design for his study, as well as on some limitations of his study.

What holds all three of these cases together is the curiosity of the teacher-researcher as the original motivating force for the research endeavor. A closely related aspect of this common theme is that, in all three cases, the teacher or teachers see themselves as the primary researchers; they may make use of other resources, but they maintain their own ownership of the study they are conducting. This emphasis on ownership is arguably the most significant way teacher-based action research differs from other, more traditional research. As Bogdan and Biklen (1992) have noted,

> Research is a frame of mind—a perspective people take toward objects and activities. Academicians and professional research-ers investigate questions that are of interest to them. They state the purpose of their study in the form of hypotheses or research questions. They are not only expected to conduct research, but are urged to do so along the lines of established research tradi-tions, whether quantitative or qualitative. While colleagues argue, they share a consensus about what it means to do research. Outside the academy, people in the "real world" also can conduct research—research that is practical, directed at their own concerns and, for those who wish, a tool to bring about social change. (p. 223)

Classroom teachers are presented with a wide range of possible research topics every day in their classrooms; many of these topics are significant and important to a teacher's own effectiveness in the class-room (see Kemmis & McTaggart, 1988; Mohr & MacLean, 1987). An important part of becoming a reflective practitioner is the ability to recognize these topics and to seek, in whatever manner seems most appropriate, to resolve them.

Propositions for Reflection and Consideration

1. No single model of inquiry includes all cases and types of edu-cational inquiry. Inquiry can be more or less formal, more or less rigorous, can involve a wide range of different techniques and methods, and can even entail very different (and some-times incompatible) ideas and assumptions about the nature of knowledge and knowing.

2. Inquiry is a dynamic rather than a static process and always takes place in a social and cultural context.
3. The individual characteristics necessary for inquiry to take place are intellectual curiosity, motivation, openness in inquiry, and openness to challenge.
4. Classroom-based inquiry should begin with a problem or puzzle that is of real concern and interest to the teacher to ensure that the teacher has ownership of the research study.
5. A school that exemplifies a culture of inquiry entails not merely teachers engaged in inquiry but also teachers and others collaboratively and collegially seeking better to understand and thus improve aspects of the schooling experience. This requires an ongoing commitment to valuing curiosity, mutual respect and support among teachers and between teachers and administrators, a willingness to try new ideas and practices, and the ability to remain open to the unforeseen and the unexpected.

VALUES, ETHICS, AND
REFLECTIVE TEACHING

*Always do right. This will gratify some people and
astonish the rest.*

Attributed to Mark Twain

*Ethics is everybody's concern. Scientific problems and
scientific theories may from time to time intrigue or
arrest all of us, but they are of immediate, practical
importance only to a few. Everyone, on the other hand, is
faced with moral problems—problems about which, after
more or less reflection, a decision must be reached. So
everybody talks about values.*

Stephen Toulmin (1968, p. 1)

ETHICAL DILEMMAS
AND THE PROFESSIONAL EDUCATOR:
FOUR CASE STUDIES

Horace Mann High School is a medium-sized, urban school
with a predominantly African American and Puerto Rican population. Although nearly 90% of the students enrolled at Horace Mann
are young people of color, all but 3 of the 32 teachers at the school are
white, as is the principal, John Anderson. The school has a generally

good reputation in the community, and Mr. Anderson has sought to encourage the teachers at Horace Mann to become more reflective about their teaching. During the school year, individual teachers in the school have, as always, been faced with a variety of ethical dilemmas and have resolved these dilemmas in different ways. Four cases in particular demonstrate the role and place of reflection in ethical decision making, and we turn now to an examination of these cases.

The Case of Maria Sanchez

James Rafferty has been a mathematics teacher at Horace Mann High School for 6 years. He enjoys teaching and has a reputation for having high expectations of his students but also for being fair and fun in class. Early in October, one sophomore, Maria Sanchez, came up to him at the end of class and asked to speak with him privately about something. James hadn't noticed any problems with Maria's work, although she had seemed a bit absentminded recently, and he gladly agreed to meet her later that day, during his free period. He hoped he might be able to give Maria some advice about whatever was distracting her and thus improve her classroom performance. Maria came to his office at the agreed-on time and told him she had been upset recently because another teacher, Mr. DeFazio, who taught social studies at Horace Mann, had been trying to get her to go out with him, and she didn't want to. James was surprised by what Maria told him because he knew Ed DeFazio very well and couldn't imagine him behaving in such an unprofessional way. He told Maria that he needed some time to think about what she had told him and asked her to come to his office before classes started the next day.

The more James thought about what he had heard, the more he doubted Maria's version of events. On the one hand, Maria might easily have misunderstood something that Ed said or could even be fabricating the whole matter to make up for her own poor academic performance. On the other hand, he was concerned that if he didn't pass on what Maria had told him to the appropriate school authorities, he could himself get into trouble later on. Still, Ed was his friend, and he thought this ought to count for a great deal in a case like this one. He certainly believed that a person was innocent until proven guilty and was afraid that if a claim of this sort were pursued, it could fairly quickly turn into a "witch hunt" that would hurt Ed unjustly.

Finally, James stopped by Ed DeFazio's classroom and asked to meet for a drink after school to discuss something. This wasn't at all unusual, and Ed happily agreed to meet James at a local bar about 4 o'clock. When they met, James told his friend what Maria had told him. Ed denied the whole story vehemently and asked James to talk with Maria again and challenge her veracity. He suggested that if a bit of pressure was put on Maria, she would "stop all of this nonsense before it all gets out of hand." Although he had some reservations about the wisdom of taking such action, James agreed to do as Ed asked.

James met with Maria the next morning as they had arranged. He indicated that he had some doubts about what she had told him, informed her that he knew Ed DeFazio very well and couldn't imagine him asking a student for a date, and told her that if she were making up all of this, she could get into a lot of trouble. Tears welled up in Maria's eyes, but she brushed them away, said that she understood and would keep quiet, and left the room. About a week later, James received word that Maria had dropped out of school. He continued to wonder whether he had done the right thing but felt confident that Maria had probably been lying, and he was glad that his friend's reputation was safe.

The Case of Glenda Griffin

Glenda Griffin was an experienced foreign language teacher who had taught French and Spanish at Horace Mann for almost 20 years. This year, as in many years past, she had agreed to take on a student teacher during the fall semester. The student teacher was Freda VanDyke, a student at Western College, who was majoring in Spanish with minors in both French and German. An excellent student with outstanding letters of recommendation, Freda was in her second week of student teaching. Thus far, all that she had done was observe Glenda teaching and give a single quiz in one of the first-year French classes. On the Thursday of the second week of student teaching, Glenda pulled her aside and told Freda that she had a doctor's appointment across town during third period. She had forgotten to request a substitute and wanted Freda to cover the third- and fourth-period classes while she was gone. Freda felt a bit uncomfortable about this but agreed because she wanted to be helpful and also because Glenda would be one of the people assigning her grade for student teaching. When Glenda got back at the start of fifth period, she made a point of reminding Freda that they needed to keep what they had done just between the two of them.

That night, as she began writing in her journal, Freda puzzled over whether to write about what had really happened in class. She didn't want to get her cooperating teacher in trouble, but at the same time, she thought her supervisor should know what had taken place. It would be difficult to write the journal entry without mentioning the best part of the day—that she had had two really good classes during Glenda's absence. She finally called a friend, who was student teaching in a nearby elementary school, to discuss what had happened. Her friend clearly envied her having had control of a class all by herself but was also concerned that maybe Freda could get into trouble if she didn't report what had happened. Finally, after they discussed it for almost an hour, Freda decided to call her supervisor at home. She explained what had happened and stressed that she wasn't complaining or unhappy. Her supervisor was clearly not happy with what had taken place but said she'd let it go this time. She also told Freda that she was not, under any circumstances, to take charge of a class while Glenda was out of the building, and she also reminded Freda that she was not yet a certified teacher. Although Freda hadn't kept her word to Glenda to be quiet about what had taken place, she felt better now that her supervisor knew about it.

A Case of Cheating

Lenny Epstein was a new teacher at Horace Mann. He had taught at another local high school for 2 years, but this was his first at Horace Mann, and he wanted to make a good impression on his colleagues and superiors. Lenny had been a good student and very much wanted to be a good science teacher, although he knew that the students thought he was far too difficult. He believed, though, that he was just maintaining high standards and that if half (or more) of his students failed each grading period, it was because they weren't studying hard enough. Just before winter break, Lenny gave his earth science students, who had been studying geology all year, an especially difficult midterm examination. During second period, Lenny noticed that Frank Evans, one of Horace Mann's outstanding football players, kept fidgeting in his seat. Lenny walked over to where Frank was sitting and saw that Frank had hidden notes up his shirt sleeve. Lenny picked up his test paper and told him that he was done and should go to the school office and wait for him there. Frank, looking very depressed, did as he was told.

After class, Lenny went directly to the office and asked to speak with Mr. Anderson. He quickly filled in Mr. Anderson on what had taken place in his class and expected him to be pleased with the vigilance. Instead, Mr. Anderson chastised him for "making such a big issue out of all of this," reminded Lenny that Frank was "a good kid" who was probably just out of his league in Lenny's class anyway, indicated that Lenny's standards were probably too high, reminded Lenny that Frank's only chance of getting into college was on an athletic scholarship, and that a failing grade could jeopardize such a scholarship. Then he asked Lenny whether he had any problems working with black students. Lenny was very surprised at Mr. Anderson's reaction and said that he'd have to think about what the principal had said. As he left the principal's office, he told Frank to go ahead to his next class.

Lenny then went to Ernie Smart's classroom. Ernie was the Science Department chairperson, and Lenny thought that no matter what happened now, Ernie had better be involved. He quickly told Ernie, and Ernie agreed to meet him at the end of the school day in the cafeteria. Ernie was fairly supportive, to Lenny's relief, and had brought with him a copy of the National Education Association's (NEA) "Code of Ethics for the Education Profession." He pointed out one passage in particular to Lenny: "The educator shall not on the basis of race, color, creed, sex, national origin, marital status, political or religious beliefs, family, social or cultural background, or sexual orientation, unfairly grant any advantage to any student." Ernie told Lenny that he had behaved appropriately in his class and that it would be unreasonable for him to do anything except what he would do for any other student. Given his past behaviors in the classroom, Lenny would have to fail Frank for the grading period. Ernie promised to support him in the matter.

That night, Lenny went over in his head his own teaching behavior, his attitudes about athletes, about black students, and about both Frank and Mr. Anderson. The more he thought, the less sure he was that he was completely free from biased or prejudiced behavior or attitudes in his classes. At the same time, Frank had been cheating, and in any other case, he would fail the student. Finally, Lenny decided that Ernie was right and that he would have to accept the consequences of giving Frank a failing grade for the grading period.

The Case of Andrew McLaughlin

Jane Heugh has taught at Horace Mann for 5 years and is generally acknowledged to be one of the better teachers in the English Department. She is popular with both the students and her colleagues and cares deeply about what happens to the students at Horace Mann. Although Jane has a great deal of respect for many of her colleagues, the teacher with whom she has worked the most during the past 5 years has been Andrew McLaughlin. Andrew has been a public school English teacher for 37 years and believes himself still to be in his prime. Although he no longer bothers with lesson plans and uses the same handouts and tests he was using when Jane started teaching, Andrew has repeatedly told Jane that he is as up-to-date and hardworking as he was when he began teaching. Unfortunately, Jane has begun to have more and more doubts about Andrew's competence. From her perspective, Jane believes that Andrew has simply decided to "retire in place" and has long since ceased to offer his students the quality of instruction to which Jane believes they are entitled.

Because of departmental politics, Jane has thus far kept her opinions to herself. After all, she has argued, she is not the person responsible for evaluating Andrew's performance, nor has she actually seen him teach. She thinks that Andrew is outdated and out of touch; she very much doubts that students in his classes learn very much, but she isn't sure that this gives her the right (let alone the duty) to make an issue of his competence. Despite her silence, Jane has become aware of a growing barrier between Andrew and herself and suspects that he must be cognizant of her concerns. She has discussed the situation with friends who teach at other schools but has not mentioned her feelings to anyone at Horace Mann. Her friends at other schools have been sympathetic and have talked about similar situations in their own schools, but they have advised her simply to wait out Andrew's retirement, which will, after all, come within the next few years. So, although she is bothered and annoyed by the situation, Jane has continued to keep her reservations to herself and to avoid any direct confrontation with Andrew. She isn't happy with this solution but can't think of any viable alternatives.

Analysis and Discussion. In each of these four cases, an individual is presented with an ethical dilemma. The dilemmas are very different in terms of their subjects, their relative importance, and the ways they are resolved. Further, the ethical decisions made by the four individuals involved vary considerably with regard to the quality of the judgments made. All four cases share some common features as well, however, and we begin by discussing these common features.

First, in each case a real *dilemma* is present. Very often, people talk about moral or ethical "dilemmas" in situations in which most of us would have no problem at all deciding what to do. These are not actually dilemmas in any meaningful sense. A dilemma is an instance in which we do not wish to accept *any* of the possible options. In other words, a true dilemma exists only when we are choosing among undesirable choices. There are, in short, no "good" solutions or "right" answers; rather, there are only more or less "good" or "right" solutions. James Rafferty is torn between his obligations toward a student who may have been sexually harassed by a teacher and his feelings for his friend and colleague Ed DeFazio. Similarly, Freda VanDyke is torn between what she sees as both personal and professional obligations and a promise she made to her cooperating teacher. Lenny Epstein is torn between his own professional standards (as well as the NEA "Code of Ethics for the Education Profession") and pressure from his principal. Finally, Jane Heugh is torn between her concerns about a colleague she believes to be no longer competent and her belief that his problems are really not her business. In other words, in each case presented here the central figure feels torn by conflicting obligations, desires, or beliefs.

Second, in each of these four cases each person attempts to discuss his or her ethical dilemma with another person to help clarify and resolve it. Further, with the exception of James Rafferty, each of the educators involved has turned to one or more individuals outside the actual dilemma itself. Thus, Freda VanDyke turned first to a friend and then to her university supervisor. Lenny Epstein, after his problematic meeting with the principal, went to his department chairperson, Ernie Smart, for advice. Jane Heugh discussed her concerns with friends who teach at other schools. By discussing the dilemma that faces them with a presumably neutral third party, each of these three individuals increased the likelihood of making a sound ethical judgment. In contrast, James Rafferty discussed his dilemma only with Ed DeFazio—the key figure, in many ways, in the dilemma. As a consequence, he ended up making a judgment that most of us would consider highly questionable at best and, more probably, downright unethical.

Third, in each of the four cases we have examined, the individual involved did not rush to make a decision, but rather attempted to take a reasonable amount of time to make a sound and well-informed decision. Even though one may have reservations or even objections to the decisions that each of the four people made (as we ourselves do), it is clear that each one did agonize about his or her dilemma and that each did try to resolve the dilemma in the best way he or she could. In other words, all four individuals did actually engage, to some extent, in reflection about their ethical dilemmas. This is an important point because it reminds us that reflection, whatever its many benefits (and it does have many benefits, we believe), does not and cannot guarantee that our decisions and judgments will always be the right ones.

Last, these four cases make evident a claim offered some years ago by Richard Peters (1966), a British philosopher of education, who argued this:

> [Today] there are no set systems of teaching and no agreed aims of education; there is constant controversy about the curriculum and a welter of disagreement about how children ought to be treated. In more settled times only the very reflective teacher was led to probe behind the tradition for a rationale for what [she or] he ought to do; nowadays it is only the lazy or dogmatic teacher who can avoid such probing. Neither can the modern teacher find in the appeal to authority much more than a temporary resting place; for authorities disagree, and on what grounds is the advice of one rather than another to be heeded? The unpalatable truth is that the modern teacher has no alternative to thinking out these matters for [herself or] himself. Teachers can no longer be merely trained; they have also to be educated. (p. 23)

Ethics and ethical decision making, in short, is simply a part of teaching, and the classroom teacher could no more ignore or avoid ethical and moral dilemmas than he or she could avoid curricular or methodological decisions. In each of the four cases presented, the ethical dilemma that occurs is brought about by factors largely beyond the individual's control and yet must be addressed by the individual.

With these four cases in mind as background, we turn now to a discussion of the relationship of opinions, preferences, and value judgments as these affect moral and ethical decision making.

OPINIONS, PREFERENCES, AND VALUE JUDGMENTS

A very common view today voiced by educators and others in our society is that all opinions are of equal weight, are equally valid, and should be equally respected. Such a view is certainly tolerant and no doubt well intentioned, but it is also, plain and simply, wrong. If you think about this claim in the context of medicine, for instance, you will see how absurd it really is. If I am suffering from a particular illness, my grandmother, the mechanic who services my car, and my physician may well all have opinions about both what ails me and what should be done about the ailment. Although I love my grandmother dearly, and although I both respect and trust my mechanic, on medical matters it would not seem to be at all reasonable for me to trust either of them instead of or in place of my physician. Now, this does not mean that in a particular case one of them might not be more correct than the physician, but the odds (as well as human reason) would still suggest that I am better off to go with the expert. As one humorous old saying goes, "The race is not always to the swift, nor the battle to the strong, but that's the way to bet." The same, of course, would apply to the building of a house, the repair of a car, or the teaching of a particular topic in the classroom. In each instance, some individuals will have greater expertise, competence, and skill than others, and it is only reasonable and appropriate to favor their opinions somewhat disproportionately. This does not mean that once we have identified the experts in a particular field, we automatically empower them to make decisions. The actual responsibility for the decision making rests with us; it is my health, my car, my house, about which I must make decisions. The same is true when we move from the arena of personal problems to social problems. As John Dewey (1927) explained:

Inquiry, indeed, is a work which devolves upon experts. But their expertness is not shown in framing and executing policies, but in discovering and making known the facts upon which the former depend. They are technical experts in the sense that scientific investigators and artists manifest *expertise*. It is not necessary that the many should have the knowledge and skill to carry on the needed investigations; what is required is that they have the ability to judge of the bearing of the knowledge supplied by others upon common concerns. (pp. 208-209)

When we turn to the area of ethical decisions and decision making, of course, the problem is in locating the relevant experts. In fact, when we evaluate ethical or moral judgments and decisions, we do so, not on the basis of expert opinion at all, but rather on the basis of the quality of the reasoning and evidence that underlie the judgment or decision (see Becker, 1973). Thus, in the case of James Rafferty, we might be very critical of both the evidentiary base on which his decision was made (which consisted of Maria's word against Ed's word), as well as on the quality of the decision-making process itself, which allowed James to establish himself as both judge and jury in a case in which he had, to some extent, a vested interest. Another important aspect involved in evaluating ethical and moral judgments and decisions has to do with the type of claim actually being offered, and it is to a discussion of the differences between *preference claims* and *value judgments* that we now turn.

Very often in conversation and discussion, we make two different types of claims that relate to ethical issues: preference claims and value judgments. Although both types of claims can be concerned with questions of right and wrong, proper and improper conduct, and so on, their logical status is quite different, and the two types of claims should not be used interchangeably. *Preference claims* are claims about what an individual speaker believes, prefers, wishes, and so forth. Thus, if I say, "I love chocolate," or "I don't believe that extramarital sex is moral," I am merely reporting on my own feelings about these matters. Such information may be interesting or even important for others to know and may help explain my own behavior. Because these are reports of my own personal preferences, however, I am under no obligation to defend them, nor do I have to offer evidence or arguments on their behalf. If my friend Midori were to announce that she did not like broccoli, she would be reporting on a personal preference. In such a context, judgments or claims of right and wrong are simply misguided. Midori is neither right nor wrong to dislike broccoli; she simply doesn't like it, and that is all there is to the matter. Finally, the only way preference claims can be judged is in terms of how well they appear to reflect the reality of the individual speaker's preferences (see Riegle, Rhodes, & Nelson, 1990, p. 18; Wilson, 1967, pp. 56-74). In other words, given that Midori has announced her dislike of broccoli, it is reasonable to assume that she would not go out of her way to order broccoli in restaurants, nor would she be likely to serve it frequently in her own home. If, on examination, we discover that she has specifically ordered broccoli on numerous occasions and, further, that she often serves herself an especially generous helping, we would have reason to doubt the claim that she dislikes the vegetable (although there are, of course, other possible explanations as well).

Value judgments also report on ethical and moral (as well as aesthetic) matters, but unlike preference claims, they are public statements that seek to suggest that others ought to agree. Thus, a claim like, "Abortion is always, under all circumstances, wrong," is not a preference claim; rather, it is a value statement that entails the implicit claim that others ought to agree with the position the speaker is advocating. Because value statements are public in nature, evidence and arguments must be offered to support them, and they can (and should) be debated in the realm of public discourse and debate. Value judgments, in short, must be justified in some manner (see Riegle et al., 1990, p. 18; Wilson, 1967, pp. 56-74). It is important to note here, however, that although value judgments must be justified, this does not mean that we will always be able to reach agreement about them. As John Wilson (1967), the British philosopher of education, has quite correctly observed, "Unfortunately we do not always agree about the criteria of method of verification appropriate to our value statements" (p. 66).

In the area of educational policy, many controversial matters are debated and argued in various forums. For example, school prayer, school choice, sex education, merit pay for teachers, and a host of other curricular, methodological, and financial matters are all current topics of dispute that entail, at least in part, ethical and moral disagreements. In such debates and disputes, value judgments play a central role, as well they should. The underlying issues are often issues of value, and it is important that we, as a community, identify and debate these issues, recognizing from the outset that not everyone will agree with the final outcome. What we *can* do, however, is to distinguish among personal preferences, value judgments, and empirical claims and respond to each type of claim appropriately. For instance, although personal preferences may well guide our individual feelings about these topics, we cannot in good conscience expect others to honor preference claims because these are not public in nature. About value judgments, we can expect debate and sometimes disagreement among reasonable people. Finally, when we can reduce a debate to empirical claims (e.g., "the distribution of condoms in secondary schools will result in a decrease in teen pregnancy"), then our debate moves from one of values to one in which resolution can be achieved without necessarily reaching an agreement on values. In short, the distinction between preference claims and value judgments, though a very significant one, is often glossed over or missed entirely in actual policy debates, and this may be one reason why policies are often less clear, cogent, and reasonable than we might wish.

COMPETING ETHICAL THEORIES AND THE EDUCATOR

Another way ethical decision making can be approached is by examining the various ethical theories that have been proposed, defended, and critiqued historically by moral philosophers and ethicists. Among the most common ethical theories are utilitarianism, egoism, relativism, and deontological theories (see Garner & Rosen, 1967; Riegle et al., 1990, pp. 55-57; Rosen, 1978). Although the study of such ethical theories is both fascinating and worthwhile, a detailed treatment of each of these different approaches to ethical decision making is not possible here. Instead, all these different ethical theories can be grouped together into two broad, general approaches—consequentialist ethical theories and nonconsequentialist ethical theories—and we limit our discussion to these two broad categories of ethical thought (see Strike, Haller, & Soltis, 1988; Strike & Soltis, 1992).

Consequentialist ethical theories focus on the results of our actions in determining their rightness or wrongness. Thus, any particular action is neither intrinsically good nor bad; rather, it is good or bad only in some context. On such an account, telling a lie might, in some cases, be the ethically correct course of action. For example, if you have a child in your class for whom you feel a certain antipathy (which, as a committed educator, you have naturally tried to control), and the child comes up to you one day and says, "You really don't like me, do you?" many teachers would agree that, in this case, telling a lie might be preferable to telling the truth. From a consequentialist perspective, one would be obligated to consider the results of one's actions, rather than to look at the actions in a context-free manner. Further, from a consequentialist perspective, "motives are not relevant to the rightness of actions but only to the goodness of persons" (Rosen, 1978, p. 99).

The best-known example of a consequentialist ethical theory is *utilitarianism*, which basically advocates that one should seek those policies and actions that will result in the "greatest good for the greatest number." Although such an approach has initial plausibility and appeal, be aware that, in practice, it can sometimes lead us to very strange and morally problematic outcomes. It is possible, for instance, to describe a situation in which a utilitarian approach would require us to argue that the establishment of a society based on human slavery might be an ethical option—an outcome with which most of us would have very serious problems. Similarly, as Strike and Soltis (1992) describe, a utilitarian approach might lead us to agree that torture might be morally acceptable:

> Let us imagine that a dozen sadistic people have had the good fortune to have captured a potential victim. They are debating whether or not it would be right to spend a pleasant evening torturing their captive. One of the group argues in the following way: "We must admit that by torturing this person we will cause a certain amount of pain. But think how much pleasure we will give ourselves. And there are a dozen of us. While this person's pain may exceed the pleasure of any one of us, it surely cannot exceed the pleasure of all of us. Thus, the average utility is enhanced by torturing this person. We ought to do so." (p. 14)

If a utilitarian approach would lead to such outcomes, then we need to be very careful as we consider such approaches to ethics. Something, in short, seems to be very wrong.

Nonconsequentialist ethical theories constitute the other major category of ethical and moral theories. Nonconsequentialist ethical theories presuppose some sort of universal moral or ethical principle or principles that should guide all behavior regardless of the consequences of a particular action in a single context. Thus, if telling a lie is wrong, it must be wrong in all possible contexts. The Ten Commandments are, basically, an example of a nonconsequentialist ethical theory. God did not provide Moses with recommendations or suggestions; the tablets contained *commandments*. Thus, the commandment is "Thou shall not commit adultery," not "Thou shall not commit adultery, except where the other party is willing and you are unlikely to get caught." The NEA's "Code of Ethics for the Education Profession," which was referred to in the case of Lenny Epstein (and which is reprinted in Strike & Soltis, 1992, pp. ix-xi), also provides an example of a collection of principles that do not appear to allow for a great deal of situational flexibility (although they do provide a bit more flexibility than the Ten Commandments). Nonconsequentialist ethical theories entail three related features:

1. The moral or ethical principle involved must be a genuine, universal principle.
2. The moral or ethical principle involved must be applied impartially; that is, it must apply to all people.
3. The moral or ethical principle must be applied consistently, and the related moral judgment involved in its application must be consistent. (Strike & Soltis, 1992, pp. 15-16)

As with the case of consequentialist ethical theories, nonconsequentialist ethical theories also have some problems. Perhaps the most troubling aspect of most nonconsequentialist ethical theories has to do with where the universal principles come from. One can address this problem theologically, of course, as in the case of the Ten Commandments, but such an approach has limited force in a secular society. The German philosopher Immanuel Kant provided an alternative way of thinking about universal ethical principles, based on what he called the *categorical imperative*. In essence, the categorical imperative is the universal principle, or rule, by which one can test all other ethical or moral rules on which one might take action. In other words, the idea underlying the categorical imperative is that "the practical or moral law as such is strictly universal; universality being, as it were, its form. Hence all concrete principles of conduct must partake in this universality if they are to qualify for being called moral" (Copleston, 1960, p. 117). In any case, it is clear that we do not yet possess anywhere near a unanimity of opinion about the origin and nature of such universal principles, and this lack of unanimity is a serious problem for nonconsequentialist ethical theories. There is an additional problem here as well because it is sometimes the case that two or more ethical principles on which we have reached agreement can, in actual practice, conflict. This is a common problem with the NEA's "Code of Ethics for the Education Profession," the Ten Commandments, and, indeed, for any ethical code, as we shall see.

CARING AND THE PROFESSIONAL EDUCATOR

An alternative and potentially quite powerful way to conceptualize the moral and ethical aspects of teaching is to think about the role of caring in the educational process in general, and in moral education in particular. This area has been extensively explored by feminists, most notably the philosopher of education Nel Noddings, who has argued "that caring is the very bedrock of all successful education and that contemporary schooling can be revitalized in its light" (1992, p. 27). Noddings's argument is grounded in the problem of the appropriate role of moral principles. Critiquing the Kantian and rule utilitarian approaches to ethics, which place moral principles at the core of ethics and ethical decision making, Noddings (1995) suggests instead that the core of morality must be the "ethic of care," which

> gives only a minor place to principles and insists instead that ethical decisions must be made in caring interactions with those affected by the discussion. Indeed, it is exactly in the most difficult situations that principles fail us. Thus, instead of turning to a principle for guidance, a carer returns to the cared-for. What does he or she need? Will filling this need harm others in the network of care? Am I competent to fill this need? Will I sacrifice too much of myself? Is the expressed need really in the best interest of the cared-for? (p. 187)

Thus, what the "ethic of care" really does is emphasize the moral interdependence of people, rather than focus on the individual as a moral agent. For educators, such a proposal has significant implications, as Noddings has explained:

> The ethic of care rejects the notion of a truly autonomous moral agent and accepts the reality of moral interdependence. Our goodness and our growth are inextricably bound to that of others we encounter. As teachers, we are as dependent on our students as they are on us. (1995, p. 196)

The ethic of care, when implemented in classroom practice (especially in terms of moral education), has four major components: modeling, dialogue, practice, and confirmation (see Noddings, 1984, pp. 171-201; 1992, pp. 22-26; 1995, pp. 190-196). Each of these components is an essential aspect of the practice of the ethic of care, and although not dissimilar to ideas found in other approaches to moral education, these components do have very specific and specialized meaning in the context of an ethic of care. Thus, *modeling* care is basically our way of showing students what care is and what it means to care, whereas *dialogue* allows us to engage our students in discourse about caring. As Noddings (1995) notes, "dialogue is such an essential part of caring that we could not model caring without engaging in it" (p. 190). *Practice* is concerned not merely with engaging in caring behavior, but even more, with the creation of a set of caring attitudes and mentalities that will, in turn, promote caring behavior. Finally, *confirmation* refers to the need to affirm and encourage the best in others, not in a sloganistic or simplistic manner, but rather through long-term relationships grounded in trust. The key here is the mutual respect necessary for the caring relationship to be possible: "One must meet the other in caring. From this requirement there is no escape for one who would be moral" (Noddings, 1984, p. 201; see also Campbell et al., 1995).

The challenge of caring, however, is a complex one. As Joseph Watras (1999) has noted:

> The ideal of caring is an ambiguous slogan . . . the general proposal that teachers and administrators should demonstrate a caring attitude is trivial, vague, or indeterminate. As a result, it is open to misuse. For example, school administrators could hold teacher in-services on caring in order to reduce teacher stress instead of offering more expensive alternatives such as

reduced class size. However, such criticisms overlook the ways that philosophers use the idea of caring. . . If teachers spent more time considering the implications [of the concept of caring] about the role of the teacher, the aim of education, and the proper curriculum, they might think more deeply about their jobs. Such caring teachers might improve schools. (p. 83)

In other words, caring, like other positive educational values, only makes sense in the more general context of reflective practice.

THE ROLE OF REFLECTION IN ETHICAL PROFESSIONAL PRACTICE

Given the discussion of consequentialist and nonconsequentialist ethical theories, their problems and limitations, and, of course, the essential issues of nurturing and caring as functions of the educator, what are we left with? Certainly, we are left somewhat frustrated, and perhaps irritated, because it is clear that no easy solutions or techniques exist for resolving ethical dilemmas quickly and painlessly. At the same time, our discussion thus far should make clear why a chapter on ethics is necessary in a book concerned with reflective practice. Ethical decisions and decision making are inevitably a necessary part of teaching, as we have seen, and at the same time ethical decision making is as resistant to "cookbook" types of approaches as are other aspects of good teaching. In short, the same kinds of concerns and considerations that affect reflective practice in general will affect ethical decision making in particular.

Perhaps most important in making ethical and moral judgments in the classroom is the need to recognize that such judgments are not merely matters of personal opinion and preference; they are, rather, judgments, and as such must be publicly defended and supported. Further, it is important to keep in mind an important difference in some cases between what the institutional rules and regulations (or even the law itself) dictate and what we may believe to be ethically or morally correct. The better our reasoning, the better our ethical decisions. This does not, of course, mean that all our ethical decisions and judgments will be perfect, but it does mean that we will have done our best and will have made the greatest possible use of the resources available to us in making our decisions and judgments. As Donald Vandenberg (1983) has argued:

> The ethical problems of educational practice ought therefore be reasoned through with as much objectivity as possible. This means that the questions of pedagogy should be considered as moral questions and reasoned through in terms of universal obligations expressed as human rights. No ethical, political, social, religious, or psychological ideology should be imposed upon these educational questions, for these are manipulative, part of the problem, and an affront to human dignity. (p. 55)

Education, in short, is an endeavor that is intrinsically ethical in nature, and just as we wish to ensure that educators are competent masters of their subject matter, of the pedagogical knowledge of their craft, and of the actual methods to be used in the classroom, so too should we hope that they will be good ethical decision makers. Underlying all these hopes, of course, is the goal of the reflective practitioner.

Propositions for Reflection and Consideration

1. Ethical decisions and judgments involve real dilemmas in which one is presented with two or more undesirable options from which a choice must be made.
2. Good ethical decisions and judgments are the result of reflective interaction involving other people, preferably individuals not themselves involved in the ethical dilemma.
3. Not all opinions are of equal worth. Opinions must be judged by public criteria to determine their validity. To some extent, the opinion of an expert in his or her own field is likely to be of greater value than that of a non-expert.
4. Personal preferences and value judgments are logically and practically distinct, and only the latter should be taken into account in deciding public matters and disputes (including those in the educational realm).
5. Ethical judgments and decisions may be based on either consequentialist or nonconsequentialist ethical theories, but in either case they must also rest on public evidence and argument.

6. Ultimately, ethical judgments and decisions must be held to the same standards of evidence and rationality as other types of judgments and decisions.
7. The ethic of care provides a powerful and compelling alternative way to conceptualize aspects of both professional ethics and moral education.

DEMOCRATIC SCHOOLING, CRITICAL PEDAGOGY, AND REFLECTIVE PRACTICE

THE NEXUS OF SCHOOL AND COMMUNITY

The role of the community in making the schools vital is just as important as the role of the school itself. For in a community where schools are looked upon as isolated institutions, as a necessary convention, the school will remain largely so in spite of the most skillful methods of teaching. But a community that demands something visible from its schools, that recognizes the part they play in the welfare of the whole . . . that uses the energies and interest of its youthful citizens, not simply controlling their time until they are prepared to be turned out as citizens—such a community will have social schools, and whatever its resources, it will have schools that develop community spirit and interests.

John and Evelyn Dewey (1915/1962, p. 128)

*Indeed, it has been said that democracy is the worst form
of government except all those other forms that have been
tried from time to time.*
Winston Churchill, House of Commons,
November 11, 1947

*Democracy cannot flourish half rich and half poor, any
more than it can flourish half free and half slave.*
Felix G. Rohatyn

THE CASE OF
BROADBENT MIDDLE SCHOOL

Northport is best known as the site of the national headquarters of a large manufacturing firm, and its economy and social life have been closely intertwined with the firm for decades. In recent years, the manufacturing firm has fallen on hard times, and each year, layoffs have increased. In this environment, funding and support for the schools have been growing more and more problematic, and there is a strong movement in the community to cut drastically the school's budget.

Alice Meere is the principal of Broadbent Middle School, which is one of two middle schools in Northport. The faculty at Broadbent Middle School is composed of highly educated professionals who have been repeatedly recognized by accreditation teams for their subject matter competence. Under Alice's leadership, the faculty have willingly accepted the responsibility for developing new courses of study and academic programs and believe that they have been very successful in their efforts.

As a way of protecting Broadbent Middle School, Alice decided to hold a series of public meetings in the auditorium, where teachers, school administrators, and local political leaders would be able to present arguments and evidence about the fiscal needs of the schools in Northport. The first of these meetings took place on a Tuesday evening, and although well attended, was not quite the success on which Alice had counted.

The turnout at the Tuesday meeting was well beyond anyone's expectations, but the crowd present was far more critical of the schools than Alice or any of her staff had expected. Parents and other members of the community challenged the competence of the teachers, the content of the curriculum, the lack of adequate vocational programs, and what they perceived as exorbitant teacher and administrator salaries. It was clear that many people in the community were angry with the schools and believed that they had no input into important decisions that affected their children and the way their taxes were spent. Alice was afraid that the public meeting she had scheduled may have done far more harm than good by providing a public forum for attacking the schools, and she was unsure about what her next step should be.

Analysis and Discussion. The case of Northport is far from unusual as budgets and resources are stretched to and beyond their limits. Particularly interesting in this case is how out of touch with the community the principal and teachers seem to have been. Although they no doubt anticipated that concerns would be voiced, they did not realize how angry parents and other members of the community were with a whole host of issues related to the school. Further, members of the community had come to see the school system, not as "our" system, but rather as an imposed and somewhat alien system controlled by professionals that was costing them a great deal of money and not providing the services they desired. In other words, the school-community bond in Northport had been effectively severed. The challenge facing Alice Meere and her staff, as well as other educators in the school system, is less the immediate problem of the budget than the more general and far more significant problem of developing support in the community.

THE SCHOOL-COMMUNITY INTERFACE

Until the last quarter of the 19th century, the family was the major socializing force in the lives of its members. A wide variety of functions were provided for, to a significant degree, by the family: business (the home was the center of work for most Americans), education (parents were responsible for the education of their children), vocational training (children received job training from their parents), religion (families supplemented the church both in terms of religious instruction and religious practice), correction (families were responsible for disciplining their members), and welfare (care was provided for all members, young and old) (see Demos, 1970). As American society became increasingly urbanized and industrialized and as the population of the society became more diverse, state governments gradually began to view education as a means of carrying out a variety of social agendas. The emergence of tax-supported, public educational systems, initially in New England and rapidly spreading through the Old Northwest, led to important questions about the role, nature, and purposes of such educational institutions. Among the more significant questions with which Americans were faced were: What is the role of education in a democratic society? What are the purposes of the existing reading and writing schools, the academies, and the grammar schools? Should the schools maintain the status quo and preserve the groups controlling society? Or, rather, should the schools be charged with the responsibility of improving the general welfare of all the people? These questions had actually been implicitly addressed earlier in American history by no less a figure than Thomas Jefferson, who was the first American leader to seek to "establish public education as an instrument for the realization of democracy and for furthering social reform," (Sizer, 1984, p. 71). More important for our purposes here, these same questions are still being debated in the 21st century. As teachers, administrators, parents, and other citizens seek to come to grips with such questions, they need to reflect on their own values, determine individual and group positions, and then develop the kinds of schools and schooling that will meet not only the wants and aspirations of the youth in their classrooms but also the needs of the society.

TOWARD A CRITICAL PEDAGOGY

Freire (1973, 1974) has discussed the conservative role played by the school in a slightly different context. He argues that dominant cultures (e.g., in contemporary U.S. society, the Anglo American culture) tend to overlook the wants and needs of the dominated cultures that coexist with the dominant culture. Freire suggests that schools, as social institutions involved in the maintenance of the status quo, generally function to impose the values of the dominant culture on dominated cultural groups in the society. Basic literacy skills, such as reading and writing, can sometimes thus become for dominated groups acts of memorization and repetition, rather than acts of reflection on meaning and critical translation into a child's own culture.

This need not be the case, of course, and when the latter takes place, education becomes transforming, not only to individuals but also for both the dominant and dominated cultures (see McLaren & Leonard, 1993). Although such transformative educational experiences remain relatively uncommon, they have received significant support and attention in U.S. public education, especially among those who consider themselves advocates of "critical pedagogy" (e.g., see Giroux, 1991, 1992a, 1992b, 1994, 1997a, 1997b). Peter McLaren (1989) notes:

> A radical theory of education has emerged in the last fifteen years. Broadly defined as "the new sociology of education" or a "critical theory of education," critical pedagogy examines schools both in their historical context and as part of the existing social and political fabric that characterizes the dominant society. Critical pedagogy poses a variety of counterlogics to the positivistic, ahistorical, and depoliticized analysis employed by both liberal and conservative critics of schooling—an analysis all too readily visible in the training programs in our colleges of education. Fundamentally concerned with the centrality of politics and power in our understanding of how schools work, critical theorists have produced work centering on the political economy of schooling, the state and education, the representation of texts, and the construction of student subjectivity. (p. 159)

In other words, critical pedagogy is really all about the recognition that schooling is an intrinsically *political* activity and that efforts to present it as "objective" or "neutral" are not only misguided but fundamentally dangerous. To be sure, schooling can be used to promote democracy and democratic values (see Gutman, 1987), but it can be (and often is) also used to perpetuate an unjust and inequitable status quo. As Henry Giroux (1992a) has explained, "Central to the development of critical pedagogy is the need to explore how pedagogy functions as a cultural practice to *produce* rather than merely *transmit* knowledge within the asymmetrical relations of power that structure teacher-student relations" (p. 98).

With this background in mind, we turn now to case studies in which the relationships between schools and their communities play a central role in both the promotion of social change and the perpetuation of the status quo.

THE CASE OF THE
FENTON PUBLIC SCHOOLS

Fenton is a city of 30,000 people on Sebastian Bay, 200 miles northwest of the state capital. It is the only city in Fenton County, and its schools are reasonably well funded by state standards, being above average in the per pupil state equalized valuation (SEV) as a consequence of the presence of a large cement factory, several lumber mills, and various other businesses located in Fenton, which is the center of commerce and banking in the county. In addition to the city of Fenton, five rural townships are in the county, all relatively poor in comparison with Fenton. The five townships all rely for educational funding primarily on their agricultural base. Each of the townships supports a relatively modern K-8 school, and all high school students in the county attend either Fenton High School or St. Michael's, the local parochial high school. The construction of the five township elementary schools has created a high level of school debt for each township. The K-8 programs in the township schools are relatively weak because of the inability to attract quality teachers, low per pupil expenditures, and, at least according to many teachers in these schools, relatively low educational expectations on the part of parents for their children.

Fenton High School has an enrollment of 1,300 students—700 from the city and 600 from the townships. Over the years, a comprehensive educational program has been developed that has met the perceived needs of the students from the city as well as the townships. Of particular note are the college preparatory and vocational education programs. Both are tied to programs at the Fenton Community College, which is part of the state community college system.

Until recently, Fenton High School has had sufficient space to provide quality education for the wide range of city and township students. Faced with increasing enrollments, though, the Fenton Board of Education has decided that if the present programmatic depth and breadth, to which parents have become accustomed, is to be continued, a new high school must be built. Because the new high school would be built primarily to serve the increasing numbers of students from the townships (the projected number of students from Fenton showing no growth), the board of education is aware of the possible resistance from Fenton residents, many of whom would have serious reservations about paying for a new high school for the children of township residents.

The superintendent of schools studied the situation and recommended that the board of education ask each of the five township school boards to schedule a vote to approve annexation to the Fenton Public Schools, thereby ensuring the enrollment at Fenton High School. In return for giving up control over its elementary school, the Fenton Public Schools would assume the school debt of each township, bring the physical plants and school staffs up to the standards of the Fenton Public Schools, and agree to appoint one member from the five township school boards to the Fenton Board of Education. After much public discussion and debate, the townships agreed to call for the vote. Much to everyone's surprise, each of the townships voted overwhelmingly in favor of annexation, and the Fenton Public Schools grew from 3,000 to 6,000 students and from an area of 12 square miles to 550.

Realizing that, with the vote, school-community relations had changed drastically and that five predominantly rural communities were now an integral part of the city school district, the superintendent, with the approval of the board of education implemented a community school program. The program was designed to provide each elementary school in the new school district school with a formal decision-making process and a means of communication with the central administration and governing bodies. The community school program had three objectives:

1. To provide the youths and adults of a school with after-school recreation programs
2. To provide adult education courses at the school

3. To provide a process by which the principal, teachers, and parents were responsible for managing their school, by which members of a school community could discuss their wants and needs and by which requests for action could be transmitted to either the school board or city council, whichever was appropriate

Analysis and Discussion. The Fenton Public Schools had more than an educational problem when annexation was approved by the five township school districts. The effectiveness and efficiency of the new school district would depend to a large degree on the process of value generation in the five townships, as well as in the city of Fenton itself. All organizations and citizens would be a part of that value generation, either consciously or unconsciously. The school leadership needed to find a sense of shared values or had to help create it. There were shared values when the townships were independent, but new values would supplant them as new interactive relationships came into being. The superintendent, however, was concerned that when the new school district was created, township autonomy might become dependent on the city of Fenton, creating a negative relationship of the sort described by Freire.

The superintendent realized that the new value system generated would be crucial to success. As Gardner (1990) has written,

> If it is healthy and coherent, the community imparts a coherent value system. If it is fragmented or sterile or degenerate. Lessons are taught anyway—but not lessons that heal and strengthen. It is a community and culture that hold the individual in a framework of values; when the framework disintegrates, individual value systems disintegrate. (p. 113)

The township communities were homogenous and traditional in nature and experienced little change from one generation to the next, whereas the newly created Fenton School District was heterogeneous and now was confronted with the likelihood of rapid change.

As a result, the superintendent recommended to the school board a community school program similar to that developed by the Mott Foundation from 1930 to 1980 (see Totten, 1970). The program provided a means for parents, teachers, students, and citizens to meet for recreational, educational, social, and political purposes.

Understandably in the Fenton case, however, more emphasis was placed on the third objective. Theoretically, it would provide each school community with the power to manage its own school, as well as affect the Fenton School Board and its own township government. Similarly, the Mott Community Schools Program envisioned that social agencies, churches, governmental units, service clubs, families, labor and industrial groups, communication media, and any other groups would contribute to the community school (Totten, 1970, p. 4). Such contributions would help achieve the following "anticipated outcomes" for both the community and individuals residing in the community:

- Better understanding of social trends
- Reduction of poverty
- Improved cultural tone
- Reduction of school dropouts
- Improved health and safety
- Reduction of delinquency and crime
- Better employment
- Improved level of literacy
- Other individual and community improvement

The school would thus be the "catalytic agent" in accomplishing the shared purposes of the community. The role of the school itself was expanded to include the following functions:

- Expectant mothers receive instruction in prenatal care and in planning for parenthood.
- Infants receive health checkups of a clinical nature.
- Preschool children get ready for the experience of kindergarten.
- Undernourished children receive wholesome breakfasts.
- Children and youths, during optional periods, engage in a variety of enrichment activities, give expression to their creative talents, and engage in wholesome cultural, social, recreational, and service activities.
- School dropouts are reclaimed through personalized programming.
- Some adults learn to read, write, and acquire other basic skills, and other adults study in the fields of learning of their choice.

- Men and women displaced by automation or forced to rely on public aid can retrain and acquire new marketable skills
- Mothers learn how to purchase, prepare, and conserve food economically, as well as to construct, repair, and launder clothing
- Referrals are made to other agencies for help with specific needs
- Community leaders are discovered and developed
- People of all races and all socioeconomic backgrounds work, study, and play together on an equal basis
- Older citizens are reclaimed and learn that they are still needed (Totten, 1970, pp. 6-7)

The community school program implemented in the Fenton Public Schools was an attempt to reach out and develop new interactive relationships between the public schools and their communities—one that would create a positive and supportive value structure for the new school district.

THE CASE OF
CENTRAL CITY MIDDLE SCHOOL

The Central City Middle School had been the old high school prior to the construction of the new high school. Modifications for a middle school had been made in the old structure, but 40 years of being "the" high school were too much to overcome. Now 900 students attended classes in a building designed to hold 1,200. The building was more than adequate, but many of the homes in the surrounding community were run-down and had been converted to multifamily occupancy. Several high-rise tenements had been constructed during the last several years. City reports described the area as lower socioeconomic status, with a rising crime rate.

One day, teachers at Central City Middle School were talking animatedly in the teachers' lounge about how difficult it was to teach the students in their classrooms. The discussion touched on a myriad of problems: single-parent families, drug addiction, teenage pregnancies, child abuse, the never-ending need to discipline, the lack of student motivation, unconcerned parents, low attendance at

PTO meetings, and so on. Peter said he thought that Central City Middle School was becoming a fortress in the middle of a hostile neighborhood. Halimah agreed with the shopping list of problems but added that she thought the safest part of each 24-hour day for the students was when they were in school. George said the growing number of problems almost made it appear that parents did not care for their children and their education. Peter disagreed, arguing that perhaps just as the teachers needed help with all the problems swirling around each of the students that affected their behavior, so too the parents needed help. Just at that moment, a counselor, who had been listening attentively, challenged the group by asking them to sit down and talk the situation over with some parents and other members of the community. When the issue was presented to the principal, she was supportive and put the issue on the agenda for the next faculty meeting. Although many teachers did not think that scheduling meetings with parents and community representatives would work, others thought the idea might help the middle school program and agreed to give the meetings a try. The principal supported the idea strongly and indicated that she would help set up the meetings.

Analysis and Discussion. Many times, the reluctance of parents to become involved with teachers in trying to address their children's school problems is the result of the negative school experiences the parents themselves had as children. Still, the enthusiasm of some teachers to attempt to work with the parents of their students could be the first step to restructuring a school perceived by some faculty as a "fortress in the middle of a hostile neighborhood." It is important to note, as this case makes clear, that one does not need unanimous support for an effort to change the school environment; rather, one only needs the support of a core group of committed individuals willing to give change a chance. The principal's supportive role is often a key facet in such efforts because the principal will most likely provide communication with and be able to gain support from the central office, as well as provide administrative assistance of various sorts. James Comer (1980), of Yale University, has strongly advocated the need for school personnel to work with parents to "reduce communication and interpersonal problems" (p. 67). He has suggested that, too frequently, when teacher-parent groups do meet, there is no agreed-on problem solving mechanism. Consequently, in attempting to resolve a problem without guidelines, chaos often reigns and mistrust grows, ultimately destroying what started out as a positive effort.

In Comer's (1980) own work with urban schools, specific program goals were identified:

- To modify the climate—social and psychological—of the school in a way that facilitates learning
- To improve the achievements of basic skills, particularly reading and mathematics, at a statistically significant level
- To raise motivation for learning, mastery, and achievement in a way that will increase academic and occupational aspiration levels of each child
- To develop patterns of shared responsibility and decision making among parents and staff
- To develop an organizational relationship between child development and clinical services at Yale University and the educational programs in school systems (pp. 67-68)

To achieve these program goals, Comer established a general process, which he has implemented in several school districts, to bring parents into the decision-making process of the school. This process might, for instance, include the following steps in a particular setting:

1. To hold an orientation workshop in the summer for parents, teachers, and administrators to establish positive relationships and trust
2. To have the workshop participants discuss and analyze school problems and gain common perspectives
3. To have workshop participants discuss school governance as a process for planning, implementing, and evaluating programs
4. To establish an overall steering committee of teachers, parents, and administrators "to improve the climate of relationships between parents and school staff, among school staff . . . between staff and students, and to improve teaching and curriculum, staff selection and program evaluation"
5. To ask parents and teachers to plan social activities to support the school program
6. To establish a mental health team to help teachers manage children with discipline problems

7. To develop and implement programs devised by parents and teachers to resolve various school problems (Comer, 1980, pp. 72-73)

The teachers in Central City Middle school might use similar steps to establish effective working relationships with their parents. In any case, the teachers would be extending the school into the community and, in turn, bringing parents into a meaningful relationship with teachers and administrators.

THE CASE OF JAMIE HENDERSON AND THE PINK TRIANGLE

Jamie Henderson has been a successful biology teacher at West Columbus High School for the last 5 years. West Columbus is a fairly conservative suburban community, and relations between the school and the community have been quite good historically. When she first moved to West Columbus, Jamie was somewhat concerned about the conservative nature of the community, especially because she knew that she would be teaching evolutionary theory as part of the curriculum. Much to her surprise, parents and colleagues had been very supportive of the curriculum, and the chairperson of the board of education had even been quoted in the local newspaper defending the need to expose students to important theories and perspectives whether or not one actually agreed with them personally. Jamie has been recognized as a good teacher and has been popular with students, colleagues, and parents. After 5 years in West Columbus, Jamie feels at home and comfortable in her environment.

The past summer was a somewhat dramatic one for Jamie's family. Her younger sister, Irene, decided to "come out of the closet" and announced at a family gathering that she was a lesbian and was living with another woman. Jamie's family was deeply divided by the news, and many relatives made it clear that they would have nothing more to do with Irene. Jamie was very upset to see how her sister was treated during and after the gathering, and she spent a good deal of time trying to sort out her own feelings on the matter. Jamie became her sister's staunchest defender in the family and, as a result of her experiences, decided that it was important for her to provide support for any of her students who might be homosexual.

At the start of the school year, Jamie posted a pink triangle on the door to her classroom and explained, in each of her classes, that it meant her classroom was a "safe zone" in which students could feel comfortable discussing issues of sexuality and sexual preference. She told her students about her experiences with Irene and tried to make it clear that she would be nonjudgmental and supportive of anyone who wanted to discuss issues of this sort with her. She also indicated that she expected all students in her classes to respect others' rights to discuss these issues in a mature manner.

Jamie thought that she had acted in a proper, professional, and ethically correct manner, but she soon discovered that many colleagues and parents did not share this view. The visual image of the pink triangle, coupled with her comments in class, quickly made Jamie a topic of considerable controversy in the school district. Many parents and some of her colleagues believed that she was actually advocating immoral behavior, supporting a "militant gay agenda," and even trying to recruit students to a homosexual lifestyle. The issue was debated in letters to the editor in the local newspaper and was the focus of an angry board of education meeting in early October at which the superintendent was directed by the board to set up a special meeting between the board, Jamie, and some parents who had complained about her actions.

Jamie was obviously upset by these developments and was puzzled by what she viewed as intolerance and insensitivity on the part of the parents and the board of education. She was also disappointed in the school administration's response to the situation, which she viewed as basically noncommittal, and she felt both frustrated and abandoned by the administration's failure to provide the kind of leadership she believed was necessary.

Analysis and Discussion. This case is a powerful one with respect to the potential for conflict between community values and school values (or at least of parts of the school community). In a culturally diverse society such as our own, it is inevitable that value conflicts will occur on many issues. In the case of Jamie Henderson, we have a teacher who is honestly and sincerely attempting to provide what she believes to be a tolerant and supportive environment for her students. At the same time, many in the community find the toleration that

Jamie is advocating to be offensive and an affront to deeply held religious beliefs. To some extent, this situation could be ameliorated by open and honest discussion about what Jamie was trying to accomplish (and perhaps more important, what she was *not* trying to accomplish), but it is unlikely that an immediate solution will be acceptable to all parties involved. This is an instance in which no consensus is reached between the school and the community on an important social, cultural, and educational issue. Whether a consensus can be reached in this case is highly debatable, but it is clear that ongoing discussion and communication are needed, as indeed is effective leadership from both the school administration and the board of education.

THE SCHOOL AND THE COMMUNITY: SOME CONCLUSIONS

For too long a period of time, the educational problems confronting the United States and its 14,000 school districts have been perceived as fundamentally school problems. Consequently, the attack on those problems has been made primarily by the school forces. The many other organizations, groups, and individuals that are also responsible for the problems have been denied access to decision making and problem resolution. Sarason (1990) has argued:

> To a significant degree, the major educational problems stem from the fact that educators not only accepted responsibility for schooling but more fateful, also adopted a stance that essentially said: we know how to solve and manage the problems of schooling in America. Educators did not say: there is much that we do not know, many problems that are intractable to our efforts, and many individuals we are not reaching or helping. (p. 36)

The family of the 21st century will not be solely responsible for the functions of business, education, vocational training, religion, correction, and welfare, but will share those responsibilities with community agencies. Schools cannot be solely responsible for problems affecting education from the larger society. All community groups that are also affected by those problems should participate in their discussion, analysis, and resolution. This necessitates a systems approach to problem solving by schools and school districts. Only when educational responsibility is shared can education be reformed.

Propositions for Reflection and Consideration

1. Public education is a process for achieving democracy and furthering social reform.
2. Depending on the issue, schools can assume either a conservative role (maintaining the status quo) or a progressive role (being a change agent). When schools are open to the needs and wants of students, particularly in urban areas, schools need to be progressive.
3. Teachers and administrators need to determine what the overall role the school is—conservative or progressive.
4. In effective and efficient schools, change is a dynamic, interactive process between a school and its community.
5. Shared values are generated when a school and its community interact. Those shared values undergird and strengthen schools and their programs.
6. When schools are isolated from their communities, their educational programs become ineffective and their culture begins to disintegrate.
7. Educators have accepted responsibility for problems originating in the larger society even though they do not have solutions for them. Those problems affect many other organizations as well. To generate effective and efficient solutions, educators need to use a system approach, in which other organizations share in decision making.
8. The teacher, principal, and superintendent play key roles in developing a positive role for the school in the community.

TRANSFORMATIVE AND CONSTRUCTIVIST CURRICULA AND INSTRUCTION

What the best and wisest parent wants for his own child,
that must the community want for all of its children.
                                    John Dewey (1902/1943, p. 7)

The traditional craft of the teacher can be rescued and
strengthened by understanding the connection between
the content area of the curriculum and how it will be
understood by the student. Understanding this
connection involves recognizing the cultural pattern of
thought (the episteme) that underlies the organization of
knowledge in the curriculum unit as well as the
phenomenological world of the student. The latter is
essential for grasping what the student is likely to
understand and how that understanding will be
integrated into the student's pattern of thinking.
                                    C. A. Bowers (1984, p. 78)

TOWARD TRANSFORMATIVE CURRICULA AND INSTRUCTION: THREE CASE STUDIES

Trying an Integrated Curriculum

Jack Williams is an English teacher, and Rita Lopez is a social studies teacher. Both are concerned about the 10th graders with whom they work, and are worried in particular about how many of their students will return in the fall. It is almost the end of the year, and many students are obviously discouraged and alienated by school.

Claremont High School, where Jack and Rita teach, is a school of about 1,100 students, racially and linguistically mixed, with many students coming from families in which unemployment and under-employment are major problems. Many students are not performing at grade level, as is clearly seen in the results of the state mastery test scores. The students are discouraged by a variety of factors, including not only school-based issues but also their own economic circum-stances and the economic circumstances of those around them. Although they have been told repeatedly about the value of educa-tion, they don't actually see much difference in outcome between those who drop out of school and those who stay. Many African American and Hispanic students believe that their skin color and lan-guage will bar them from any significant advances no matter what they do. Clashes have occurred between some of the different groups in the high school, a few of which have been serious. Many teachers at Claremont see the students as hostile, belligerent, and arrogant. Many students were labeled long ago as "learning disabled" or "behaviorally disordered," and these labels have continued to affect their treatment in the school.

In recent years, Claremont has been divided into four "houses," each with its own vice principal. The motivation for dividing the school this way was that the smaller groups would provide more of a sense of family and that the vice principal could get to know more stu-dents on an individual basis. To a minor degree, some of these things have occurred, but no significant effects on the students' academic achievement has occurred as a consequence of the establishment of the smaller houses in the school.

During the current school year, a faculty committee at Claremont has studied different possibilities for developing some kind of thematically structured curriculum. Themes that were discussed included the environment, global education, and multiculturalism. In their discussions, the teachers also considered interdisciplinary team-teaching approaches, as well as alternative scheduling possibilities that would allow a team of teachers to work with the same small group of students, in different subjects, for most of the day. They had initially been enthusiastic about trying such a thematic approach that would allow more in-depth and integrated treatment of topics of interest and concern to their students.

During one spring faculty meeting, the committee reported back on its work to the entire faculty. The reaction to the committee's report and suggestions was swift and angry. Some teachers took the position that "these kids can't handle that kind of curriculum complexity." Others argued that the students needed tight structures and strong discipline to keep them under control. Several teachers asserted that an integrated curriculum would inevitably water down everything and, in any event, simply pandered to students' interests. As one teacher commented, "These kids barely can say their name and maybe write it, and you want them to tackle these kinds of topics? Get real!" One teacher made an eloquent speech on the necessity of good lectures and note-taking skills as real education; he went on to note that this was essential for those few that will go on to real colleges and that, for the rest, it would be beneficial for them to learn how to pay attention. The committee's suggestions were rejected, and no follow-up was proposed.

Jack and Rita, who had both been involved in the proposal, felt hurt and defeated. A few days after the meeting, Rita suggested to Jack that they try some of the ideas the committee had recommended, on a much smaller scale, with one class of 11th graders they might share next year. They spoke with the principal, and she agreed to schedule a group of students in back-to-back classes each day and to schedule Jack and Rita for alternating free periods so that both could be involved with the same group for 2 hours each day, although it would also mean that both teachers would have to give up their one free period.

This arrangement meant they could integrate the curriculum around themes that were relevant to the lives of their students. Both Rita and Jack believed that they would be able to draw on a wide variety of sources from social studies and literature.

The methodology that Jack and Rita agreed on involves their selecting a major theme, presenting the theme in a question form to the class, and then having the students identify the smaller questions embedded inside the larger question. Readings from newspapers, journals, technical reports, short stories, essays, novels, poetry, plays, films, and various historical documents will be used, rather than the regular textbooks. Different students will accept responsibility for reading and reporting back to the class about different documents. Subgroups will decide on other ways to explore the theme as well. For example, one group might decide to interview a variety of people in the community around a set of questions they put together on the basis of their reading, discussions, and interests. Depending on the theme, some students might decide to videotape certain kinds of situations in the community; others might search out various kinds of records relevant to their investigation at the courthouse and in local libraries. Others would find pertinent information in museums of various types.

Rita and Jack agreed that they will give students room to explore a variety of avenues within each theme. The instructional "glue" that will hold the classes together will be the frequent group sessions in which individuals and small groups share what they have collected about the topic, what they think it means, and where it leads them next. Jack and Rita agreed that they will require frequent short reports summarizing the same information to ensure that the students are developing several different skills at the same time. During the course of the year, students will be encouraged both to work in small groups and to do some work on their own. All the students will be expected to keep a daily journal to allow for Rita and Jack to monitor their progress and to identify possible problems. The students will also be encouraged to use their journals to share with Jack and Rita personal feelings and reflections on their lives.

Although they know they have a great deal of planning ahead of them, both Rita and Jack are excited about next year and wish they could figure out a way to have the same group for longer than their 2 hours.

Toward an Environmental Curriculum

Yorkshire Middle School is in an upper-class district near a major U.S. city; it is the quintessential bedroom community for the upper- and near-upper levels of corporate America. Many well-to-do families in the area send their children to private schools. Although the parents of these students are not publicly active in community politics and institutions, they nevertheless wield much influence on community decisions behind the scenes, most often in the interest of keeping the local tax rates "reasonable."

When visiting schools in the district for the first time, one is struck by how much the school buildings look like those in poorer areas of the city. Repainting is sorely needed, custodial services are at a minimum, and instructional equipment is only slightly better than that seen elsewhere in the area. If one talks with the teachers at Yorkshire, however, it quickly becomes clear that an impressive number of very capable and creative teachers work here. Nonetheless, these teachers are confined by state and district demands and constraints like all other public school teachers; in fact, in some ways they are *more* constrained because of the high and narrow expectations that parents in such districts have. The pressures are enormous and often stultifying. Thus, although the curricula at Yorkshire and in many similar schools may appear to be more advanced because the reading sources and course titles are more sophisticated and the teachers are often (though by no means always) better educated than their counterparts in other systems, one commonly finds that students in schools such as Yorkshire appear to be as bored and disengaged as students in any other district. This is the reality of Yorkshire and many other districts nationwide that are often cited as beacons for other schools. Do not such claims, at root, suggest that we should take credit for genetics or assume that wealth guarantees academic achievement? What is the "boredom factor"?

Anne Jacobs and Kali Patel have worked together at Yorkshire Middle School for the past 10 years. Students always seem more engaged in their classes than they do in many other courses. Anne is an English teacher, and Kali is a science teacher. Anne is very involved in environmental issues, both locally and regionally, whereas Kali has been active in the human rights movement. They have both been active members in regional environmental groups and share a love of nature.

Anne and Kali are also very suspect in the community, primarily because they both have visibly challenged local and state environmental policies, as well as the effects of the consumer-oriented lifestyle prevalent in Yorkshire County.

Many parents have also voiced concerns about the two teachers, although no one has challenged the very real success that Anne and Kali have had with their students.

Anne and Kali have decided that they want to integrate the science and English curricula for Grade 8 around the general theme of "nature writing." Grade 8 is a review year for all subjects and therefore is often especially boring for most students. Anne and Kali believe that, by teaching science and English around the theme of nature writing, they will be able to use their own vocational and avocational expertise and interests while at the same time capturing the natural interest of students at that age. Such an approach will also provide their students with an opportunity to synthesize their skills and knowledge by using them in a creative, practical fashion. As an added benefit, students will confront their relationship with the natural world and will be asked to relate that relationship to global politics. Although Anne and Kali know that this approach may cause some students, and perhaps some parents, a degree of discomfort, they nonetheless believe that the activity will be valuable and worthwhile and that it is clearly educationally desirable.

Anne and Kali decide that they will begin with selected works from three naturalists representing different historical periods: Emerson, Teale, and Dillard. Each writer represents a different and distinct connection with the natural world, and all are superb writers. The teachers believe that these three writers are also a good selection because they present very different natural history interests while at the same time demonstrating the universality and timelessness of many environmental issues.

After devoting considerable time and energy to planning how they would accomplish this integration, Anne and Kali present their concept and plans to the principal at Yorkshire Middle School. The principal indicates that he has some reservations but agrees to allow the teachers to present their proposal to the board of education. At the next meeting of the board, Anne and Kali present their plans and are met with considerable hostility and rejection. Some board members react with concerns about how the content that Anne and Kali propose to teach will relate to the questions on the SAT; others express concern that this sort of exploration might lead to negative views about business and politicians. One board member questions the motives of the two teachers, who, she argues, were known to be active participants in "left-wing environmental groups." This board member also comments, as an aside, "Isn't strange that these two single women not only spend all their nonwork time together but now want to teach together as well?"

Refocusing the Curriculum on the Community

Redford School is located in northern New England near the Canadian border. It is in a community of about 2,200 people, including both townspeople and those living in the nearby countryside. The nearest sizable population center is a declining mill town of about 5,000 people. The population in Redford is fairly evenly divided between those of French Canadian heritage and those of old Yankee lineage. The French Canadians are mostly bilingual, except for a tiny number of elderly citizens; the Yankees are almost entirely monolingual.

The school is a single building, with separate corridors for the K-8 and 9-12 students. Altogether, Redford school has some 450 students—325 in Grades K-8, and 125 in Grades 9-12. The dropout rate is around 25%. Of the high school graduates, only 20% go to college. Very few students at Redford are likely to leave the area for employment elsewhere. Most people in the area do a variety of jobs to earn a living; nearly everyone does small-scale farming, at least enough to supply one's family and trade with neighbors. In addition, depending on one's skills, people do a variety of odd jobs, either for pay or to barter for other products or skills. Summer tourists are a major source of income. The tourists are not wealthy people coming to resorts, but rather are families coming to lake cottages, but they still provide some small economic opportunities for many people. The population of Redford is proud and literate and for the most part doesn't complain about life circumstances.

The school curriculum is fairly standard by state guidelines, but the school cannot afford vocational education programs, art, or music. The classes are about average size. The teachers, though fairly conservative in terms of teaching style and discipline, are clearly caring. Further, the teachers at Redford School are almost all from the area; this is a town where everyone knows everyone, and families and friendships go back for years and years.

Denise Goddu is the third-grade teacher at Redford. She was born, raised, and went to school in the town. She went to college at the state university, majoring in history and elementary education—a combined major, which took her 5 years to complete. She then went to teach in a suburban district in a nearby state for 5 years. Last year, she returned to teach in Redford.

Rob Shimkus is the fourth-grade teacher and has been teaching in Redford for 10 years. This has been his only teaching job since college. Rob was born and raised in another state in an urban area and had actively sought a different lifestyle, which he found in Redford.

Denise and Rob are both dedicated teachers who want learning to be more exciting and successful for their students. As they look at the curriculum and instruction for the first and second grade and at their own instruction, they are concerned about too much reliance on rote learning and sequential learning, as well as workbooks and ditto sheets. Students are generally all doing the same thing at the same time. There seems to be a lack of excitement in the students. Denise and Rob are also concerned that most instruction and curriculum materials are in English even though many of their French Canadian students are clearly struggling with the language. Most of all, they realize that they and their colleagues are not teaching students how to construct and implement their own learning; rather, the entire schooling experience consists of dependent learning. At the same time, Denise and Rob are very much aware that the parents are satisfied with the school because it is the same as it was when they were in the school.

Denise and Rob decide that they want to combine their two classes for 3 weeks and teach an integrated unit that will explore local history but in the process also involve language arts, science, mathematics, art, and some basic French. The unit will involve work outside school on a few days as well. After lengthy discussions with the principal and a meeting with the superintendent, they receive permission to proceed. First, they must get signed permissions from their students' parents because of the out-of-school experiences. Rather than just send notes home, Denise and Rob decide to hold an evening meeting to explain to parents what they intend to do and why they think the experience will be a worthwhile one for the students. The meeting is well attended. Many questions are asked, and although the parents are skeptical, they like and trust these teachers and agree to give the 3-week experiment a try.

Denise and Rob then spend a morning with their two classes together in the school auditorium and explain in general terms what they plan to do. The students have many of the same concerns as their parents; after all, what is being suggested is different from anything they are familiar with. The lure of not having to be in the school building all the time, however, is overpowering, and by the end of the morning, the students are as excited about the new experiment as their teachers.

The unit begins with gravestone rubbings in the oldest of the four local cemeteries. Denise and Rob give the students the necessary materials and instruction and tell them to look at different markers until they find one of particular interest. Each student is to do two rubbings of the same marker so that they can hang one in the classroom and use the other as a reference for the next phase of the project.

Back in the classroom, the students discuss their rubbings. They talk about what could be learned from the gravestones: how long people lived, family relationships, how many generations of the same family are present, and so on. One student in Denise's class points out that none of the names in that graveyard are of French derivation; this point leads to a long discussion of why this is so, and at the suggestion of Denise's class, the students make a second outing to another old graveyard where almost all the names are French. This, in turn, results in an extended discussion about religious differences, ethnic differences, and feelings of "separateness."

The students also discover a 3-year period in the early 1700s when many people of all ages died. This finding leads some students to visit the public library to search out local history books. The students discover that, during the 3-year period, a smallpox epidemic had occurred. This finding leads to reading and discussions with the local physician about the lack of medicines to fight disease and infection at that time. The students relate this information to the high number of birth deaths they had discovered in their rubbings and in the courthouse records.

The students also learn that their region was once a booming area for lumbering and the paper making. This leads them to research how these industries were conducted during earlier times; they soon realize that work then was much harder and more dangerous. The students wonder why these industries are no longer in their area. They learn what chemicals were used to form wood into paper and to bleach the paper. They discover that many workers were injured or killed during the logging and manufacturing. Soon they discover that many people who worked in the paper mills seemed not to live as long as other people.

During the 3 weeks of the experiment, Denise and Rob's students wrote their discoveries and observations each day. Some did paintings and drawings to represent important ideas; others took photographs. Some students became investigative reporters regarding safety protection for workers; others tried to find out where the paper industry had gone. Some wrote short stories and poems. One group tested the waters of the local river, streams, and ponds. All the students worked to find out where their families came from and when they arrived in Redford. The classes discussed the similarities and differences between French Canadians and Yankees and between Protestants and Catholics. They wondered why no people of other races and religions lived in the town.

Finally, the students and their teachers put on an exhibit in the school auditorium for the whole school and the community, showing their artwork, photography, stories, poems, science experiments, and investigative reports, topped off with a play written and produced by the students that depicted life in earlier times. The students handed out a newspaper they had written and produced that represented 1 day in the 1700s in their community; it was in a two-column design—one side in French, and the other side in English.

Analysis and Discussion. These three case studies all demonstrate the potential for curricular innovation and change but also remind us of the risks that such change can pose for the classroom teacher. These three case studies represent three levels of schooling and three quite different community settings. Very often, one common barrier to curricular and instructional innovation is that educators and members of the public erroneously assume that new approaches to curriculum and instruction are best limited to well-behaved, high-ability students—a view that was seen in the comments of some teachers at Claremont High School. A second common barrier is concerns about the impact of a new approach on college-bound students, especially with respect to SAT and ACT scores. Concerns of this type were seen both in the Claremont High School and Yorkshire Middle School cases. These two barriers are common blocks to changes in curriculum and instruction, as, unfortunately, are inappropriate personal innuendos of the kind faced by Anne and Kali.

Despite the differences in levels of schooling and community differences in the three cases presented here, the innovations proposed by the teachers have some common characteristics. In all three examples, the proposed curriculum is organized around themes and takes an interdisciplinary approach combining at least two subject matter areas. Thematic approaches of these kinds provide the opportunity for students to be more active learners and to experience a wider variety of learning strategies than would otherwise probably occur. They also give students more freedom to make determinations about what and how they learn, as well as how they will demonstrate what they have learned. Built into such an approach are chances for students to work alone, in pairs, or in small groups at various times, as well as all together in a more traditional classroom atmosphere. This flexibility allows for a balance between individual achievement and group accomplishment. Further, using such an approach means that assignments and activities can be geared to an individual student's current level of ability, interests, and so on.

Another valuable lesson found in all three cases is how the teachers abandoned the narrow confines of textbooks and moved instead to a variety of primary sources, including original works, records, and documents. Textbooks are, each of the teachers seems to have understood, only one possible source of information for students and are, in fact, arguably far from the best source if the goal is truly to engage students in the construction of their own learning. To do this, we as teachers need to learn to trust students to learn on their own, as well as in our presence. This, no doubt, will be a difficult lesson for many of us, but it is nevertheless an essential one.

A crucial issue often discussed but seldom implemented in meaningful ways in the schools is the need for students to engage their learning on matters of values and problems they confront in their lives and community. In other words, students must take ownership of what they are learning; they must be empowered as learners. The challenge for us as educators, as Dewey expressed it in *The Child and the Curriculum* (1902/1943), is to avoid the temptation to view the subject matter as something unrelated to the child:

> Abandon the notion of subject-matter as something fixed and ready-made in itself, outside the child's experience; cease

> thinking of the child's experience as also something hard and fast; see it as something fluent, embryonic, vital; and we realize that the child and the curriculum are simply two limits which define a single process. Just as two points define a straight line, so the present standpoint of the child and the facts and truths of studies define instruction. It is continuous reconstruction, moving from the child's present experience out into that represented by the organized bodies of truth that we call studies. (p. 11)

All too often, adults view learning as the result of formal, direct instruction. As one child commented in explaining why time at a camp wasn't "learning": "We don't learn anything here. Learning is when they write stuff on the board and you copy it down. We don't copy nothing down here; there aren't even chalkboards."

Although direct instruction certainly has its place in the classroom, students can learn in many other ways, some of them far more appropriate for specific topics than would be traditional methods of instruction. Certainly, we know that if we wish to change attitudes and behaviors, direct instruction is likely to be ineffective. Students must be given mature opportunities for engagement in social problem areas, such as AIDS, drugs, violence, abuse, environmental hazards, divorce, nuclear concerns, the homeless, prejudice, gender, suicide, stress, death, sex, and many other topics that are often avoided or inadequately handled in more traditional approaches to teaching and learning. Textbooks and lectures simply do not engage students, nor do students have any sense of ownership or interest when topics are presented in this manner. Rather, they must be given opportunities for critical thinking, discussion, exploration, and presentation. For teachers to make such opportunities possible for students will inevitably make many adults, both in and out of school, very uncomfortable and defensive—as was seen in two of our three case studies. Nevertheless, such value issues are at the heart of growing up, and dealing with them in a public and critical manner is the essence of a democracy. As Robertson (1992) argues,

> Concerns about the vitality of American political life, citizen apathy, growing disparities among citizens in wealth and power and conflict among racial and ethnic groups make Dewey's conception of public life attractive. Communities in which all share in the creation and enjoyment of common goods, in which each

person's flourishing is thought necessary for the full flourishing of the others and the individuality of each is respected, and in which conflicts are brought out in the open and resolved through public discourse surely are worthy goal. (p. 374)

As Dewey and others have urged, the community should have a major role in curriculum and instruction, and in each of the three cases presented here, the teachers engaged the community—sometimes successfully, sometimes (thus far, at least) not (see also Case et al., 1995).

TOWARD TRANSFORMATIVE CURRICULA AND INSTRUCTION

Many curriculum theorists and researchers have consistently noted the discrepancy among the planned curriculum, the enacted curriculum, and the experienced curriculum (e.g., see Gehrke, Knapp, & Sirotnik, 1992). The *planned curriculum* is that presented by state and local policies and curriculum guides, often constructed by committees in absentia and usually devoid of local context, except for historical events. Many people actually assume that this is what is taught. The planned curriculum is reinforced by standardized or state-produced mastery tests to ensure that teachers teach what they are supposed to teach. Further buttressing is accomplished through textbook series and workbooks. This structure is premised on the belief that curriculum is, at heart, mostly discrete skills and factual knowledge and that teachers can convey this efficiently to groups of students at the same time in the roughly the same way. Individuality, values, beliefs, and critical thinking are matters for rhetoric, but not to be practiced; instead, compliance and complacency rule. As Herbert Thelen wrote more than 30 years ago,

It is in the formulation of the problem that individuality is expressed, that creativity is stimulated, and that nuances and subtleties are discovered. It is these aspects of inquiry that give birth to new social movements and political orientations, and that are central in the emergence of insight. Yet it is precisely these aspects of inquiry that schools ignore, for they collapse inquiry to mere problem-solving, and they keep the student busy finding "solutions" to "problems" that are already formulated, externalized, depersonalized, and emotionally fumigated. The school is concerned with the student who formulates his own problems only when he is so creative with school property that he perforce enters a "counseling" relationship (on pain of dismissal. But as far as the academic work of the school goes, personal stirrings and strivings and self-discoveries have no place. In effect, what is missing is the investment of learning with personal emotion and meaning. (as quoted in Eisner, 1982, p. 8)

Often, other nations are seen as being more successful in their schools because their students seem to succeed better on standardized tests that measure factual knowledge. John Dewey, George Counts (1932), and many other educators have questioned whether such an approach is viable and defensible in a democratic society such as our own, and such concerns are, we would suggest, well heeded.

The *enacted curriculum* is what really happens in the classroom. This usually consists of a mixture of some of the planned curriculum, teacher additions or subtractions, teacher personality and interests, and student interests and abilities. Even though the planned curriculum and materials are often intended to be as "teacher proof" as possible, this intention is (fortunately, we would argue) rarely realized. Too little time and effort in the planned curriculum is directed to conceptual understanding, problem solving, and critical thinking. Reliance on curriculum materials divorces what is presented in the classroom from the day-to-day realities, fears, and hopes of student.

This brings us to the *experienced curriculum*, which is usually divorced from the lives of students and from the context in which they live. What students experience is a self-contained reality; that is, what happens in the classroom all too often has no relationship to anything else in the lives of the students. For many teachers, of course, the same is true, even though no direct relationship exists between their reality and the reality of the students. In the novel (and movie) *Being There*, as one of the characters is being mugged, his response is to keep clicking his remote control. One is tempted to ask whether much of what happens is schools is comparable to this meaningless and ineffectual clicking of the remote control. Why do we continue to persist in dehumanizing, alienating, and often meaningless practices when, in fact, we know better?

Traditional approaches to curriculum are mostly tied to subject matter divisions; most curriculum development occurs within these confines. This is convenient when the primary focus is on discrete skills and factual knowledge. It is even more efficient if we track students according to ability, as, in fact, we do. Further, as a consequence of long-held beliefs and practices related to ideas about teaching and learning, curriculum development often focuses on relatively narrow goals and objectives, particularly those that are easily measured. This means that curricular goals must be small and simple, not large and complex. Content within the confines of subject matter becomes the prime activity—what "pieces" of knowledge should be taught/learned, in what sequence, to what depth, and with how much breadth? How should this content be organized? Such are often the guiding questions that underlie curriculum development in the schools.

Most schools also opt to avoid conflict and controversy in curriculum materials and classroom topics. Although perhaps understandable from a pragmatic and political perspective, the result of avoiding controversial topics often leads to bland and banal course topics and materials and can hardly be seen as supportive of the development of independent and critical thinkers.

Instruction, in short, should not be separated from curriculum; the teaching method, the learning activities, the materials, and the individual interests, abilities, goals, and learning styles of the student are all part of the curriculum; no one of these should be separated from the other components.

At the beginning of this century, John Dewey sought to address what he believed to be the dualism of the relationship of the school and the society. As he wrote in *Moral Principles in Education* (1909/1975),

The school cannot be a preparation for social life excepting as it reproduces, within itself, typical conditions of social life. . . The only way to prepare for social life is to engage in social life. To form habits of social usefulness and serviceableness, apart from any direct social need and motive, apart from any existing social situation, is, to the letter, teaching the child to swim by going through motions outside of the water. The most indispensable

condition is left out of account, and the results are correspond-
ingly partial. (p. 14)

Such a conception of learning, as well as of the relationship between
the school and the community, provides a template for the creation of
effective, efficient, and democratic schools. Dewey saw that children
were naturally curious and that they had questions about the world
around them—and that their own world was rich with materials and
experiences that could be organized in interesting ways to pull them
toward the wonders of learning. Children could learn that they could
interact with and affect the world. This engagement would produce
citizens who were responsible and who did not see themselves as
powerless—citizens who would not be content to accept the world as
it was. Reflection and inquiry, Dewey believed, were essential for all
citizens in a democratic society, and it was the job of the school to promote such reflection and inquiry. Unfortunately, nearly a century
later, our schools still seem far from this ideal.

CONSTRUCTIVIST APPROACHES TO
TEACHING AND LEARNING

Another way in which the cases presented in this chapter might
be considered is through an *epistemological lens*—that is, by considering the assumptions that are being made by teachers, students, and
others about what knowledge actually is and how one becomes
knowledgeable. Underlying all pedagogical practice, ultimately, are
questions of epistemology. The way we think about *knowledge* and
what it means *to know* are directly and necessarily linked to all
aspects of how we teach. In recent years, some academic disciplines—most notably, mathematics and science, as well as literacy
and language arts—have begun to undergo a significant change in
the epistemology that underlies their pedagogical practice (for
science education, see, e.g., Fensham, Gunstone, & White, 1994;
Mintzes, Wandersee, & Novak, 1997; Tobin, 1993; for mathematics
education, see, e.g., Davis, Maher, & Noddings, 1990; Steffe, Cobb, &
von Glasersfeld, 1988; Wood, Cobb, & Yackel, 1995; for literacy and
language arts, see, e.g., Cooper, 1993; Kamii, Manning, & Manning,
1991; Nelson, 1996; Spivey, 1997). This change, which one might well

label a real paradigm shift (even in the face of the ubiquitous over- and misuse of that phrase), has been grounded in the growing popularity and credibility of constructivist approaches to epistemology and learning theory. Such views, as we shall see, are far from uniform and are also far from new, dating back at least some 60 years to the work of Jean Piaget (see Piaget, 1976, 1979, 1986, 1993, 1996), and on at least some accounts as far back as the work of Kant (see Boulter, 1997; Spivey, 1997, p. 6). They have nonetheless been slow to affect significantly educational thought and practice in many areas and are only now really beginning to come into their own (see Fosnot, 1996a; Grennon Brooks & Brooks, 1993). At the heart of the constructivist enterprise, as Catherine Fosnot (1993) has argued, is this idea:

> Constructivism is not a theory about teaching. It's a theory about knowledge and learning. Drawing on a synthesis of current work in cognitive psychology, philosophy, and anthropology, the theory defines knowledge as temporary, developmental, socially and culturally mediated, and thus, nonobjective. Learning from this perspective is understood as a self-regulated process of resolving inner cognitive conflicts that often become apparent through concrete experience, collaborative discourse, and reflection. (p. vii)

We turn now to a more explicit and detailed discussion of what constructivism suggests for educational thought and pedagogical practice.

Constructing Constructivism

Although constructivism has gained considerable attention in the educational literature in recent years, there is no clear definition or consensus of what is meant by the term (see Duffy & Jonassen, 1992; Forman & Pufall, 1988; Kafai & Resnick, 1996; Nicaise & Barnes, 1996; Schwandt, 1994; Steffe & Gale, 1995). As Virginia Richardson (1997b) has noted, "One cannot think of constructivist teaching . . . as a monolithic, agreed-upon concept . . . . There are fundamental theoretical differences in the various constructivist approaches" (p. 3). Indeed, debate even surrounds whether constructivism is best understood as an epistemology, an educational philosophy, a pedagogical approach, a theory of teaching, or a theory of learning (see Kaufman & Grennon Brooks, 1996, p. 234). Arguably the best articulation of the nature of constructivism in the educational literature is that of Catherine Fosnot (1996b), who compellingly suggests that:

> Constructivism is a theory about learning, not a description of teaching. No "cookbook teaching style" or pat set of instructional techniques can be abstracted from the theory and proposed as a constructivist approach to teaching. Some general principles of learning derived from constructivism may be helpful to keep in mind, however, as we rethink and reform our educational practices. (p. 29)

Such a view of constructivism essentially confirms its status as an epistemology—a theory of knowledge and learning, rather than a theory of teaching (see von Glasersfeld, 1993, pp. 23-24). As an epistemology, constructivism, in essence, entails the rejection of traditional transmission-oriented views of learning, as well as behaviorist models of learning. Instead, emphasis is placed on the individual learner's construction of his or her knowledge. Beyond this, though, constructivism assumes not only that learning is constructed but also that the learning process is a personal and individual one, that learning is an active process, that learning is collaborative in nature, and that all learning is situated (see Merrill, 1992, p. 102). In other words, constructivism offers a radically different view of the nature of the learning process—a view grounded in a rejection of what von Glasersfeld (1995a) has called the "domination of a mindless behaviorism" (p. 4). This view includes, as Fosnot (1996b) notes, some general principles of learning, including the following:

- Learning is not the result of development; learning *is* development. It requires invention and self-organization on the part of the learner.
- Disequilibrium facilitates learning. "Errors" need to be perceived as a result of learners' conceptions and therefore not minimized or avoided. . . Contradictions, in particular, need to be illuminated, explored, and discussed.
- Reflective abstraction is the driving force of learning. As meaning-makers, humans seek to organize and generalize across experiences in a representational form.

- Dialogue within a community engenders further thinking. The classroom needs to be seen as a "community of discourse engaged in activity, reflection, and conversation" . . .
- Learning proceeds toward the development of structures. As learners struggle to make meaning, progressive structural shifts in perspective are constructed—in a sense, "big ideas" . . . These "big ideas" are learner-constructed, central organizing principles that can be generalized across experiences and that often require the undoing or reorganizing of earlier conceptions. This process continues throughout development. (pp. 29-30)

It is important to stress here that constructivist epistemology is more than simply an alternative to other approaches to epistemology; it entails a rejection of some core assumptions that have been shared by Western epistemology for some 2,500 years (see Gergen, 1982, 1995). As von Glasersfeld (1995a) has argued, "the crucial fact [in understanding constructivism is] that the constructivist theory of knowing breaks with the epistemological tradition in philosophy" (p. 6), which is why it has been labeled not merely postmodernist, but *postepistemological* by some writers (see, e.g., Noddings, 1990).

Up to this point, we have discussed constructivism as a single entity, although keep in mind Richardson's (1997b) warning that it is far from monolithic. In reality, it has become fairly commonplace in discussions of constructivism to distinguish between what are often taken to be two fundamentally distinct, competing *types* of constructivism (see Cobb, 1994, 1996; Magadla, 1996). The first type of constructivism, *radical constructivism*, is fundamentally an epistemological construct that has been most clearly and forcefully advocated in the work of Ernst von Glasersfeld (1984, 1989, 1993, 1995a, 1995b, 1996). Radical constructivism has its philosophical roots in Piaget's genetic epistemology (Piaget, 1979; Sinclair, Berthoud, Gerard, & Veneziano, 1985) and is essentially a cognitive view of learning in which "students actively construct their ways of knowing as they strive to be effective by restoring coherence to the worlds of their personal experience" (Cobb, 1996, p. 34). Radical constructivism is premised on the belief that an individual's knowledge can never be a true representation of reality (in an observer-independent sense), but is rather a construction of the world the person experiences. In other words, knowledge is not something that is passively received by the learner; it is, quite the contrary—the result of active mental work on the part of the learner. Thus, from a radical constructivist perspective, knowledge is not something that can merely be conveyed from teacher to student, and any pedagogical approach that presumes otherwise must be rejected.

The alternative to radical constructivism is *social constructivism*, which has as its primary theoretical foundation the work of Vygotsky (1978, 1934/1986; see also Moll, 1990). Social constructivism, while accepting the notion that the individual does indeed construct his or her own knowledge, argues that the process of knowledge construction inevitably takes place in a sociocultural context and that therefore knowledge is, in fact, *socially* constructed. As Driver, Asoko, Leach, Mortimer, and Scott (1994) have argued with respect to science education, "it is important . . . to appreciate that scientific knowledge is both symbolic in nature and also socially negotiated . . . The objects of science are not phenomena of nature but constructs that are advanced by the scientific community to interpret nature" (p. 5).

The tension between radical and social constructivism, between the personal and the social construction of knowledge, is to a significant extent more apparent than real and, in any event, is certainly amenable to resolution on a practical level, criticisms to the contrary notwithstanding (see, e.g., Cobern, 1993; Confrey, 1995). As Paul Cobb (1996) has asserted, "the sociocultural and cognitive constructivist perspectives each constitute the background for the other" (p. 48), and von Glasersfeld (1995a) has recognized that "we must generate an explanation of how 'others' and the 'society' in which we find ourselves living can be conceptually constructed on the basis of our subjective experiences" (p. 12). Ultimately, even D. C. Phillips, a leading critic of the philosophical foundations of radical constructivism (see Phillips, 1995), has agreed:

> It is worth stressing that these philosophical issues do not have to be settled before the business of education can proceed. I suspect that von Glasersfeld and I are very close in the kinds of educational attitudes and practices that we endorse. If you are about to undergo brain surgery, you do not have to wait until surgeons reach agreement about the thorny philosophical issues surrounding the body-mind problem. Similarly, a student can manipulate geological samples without having to settle upon a defensible philosophical account about the nature of the existence of these samples. (Phillips, 1996, p. 20)

Perhaps the most reasonable way to articulate the common, shared elements of radical and social constructivism is to talk about learning as "socially mitigated but personally constructed," a formulation that, at the very least, moves us away from a strong bifurcation of radical and social constructivism and allows us to move on to a discussion of the implications of constructivist epistemology in general for teaching practice.

Constructivist Teaching

Although it is obviously important to keep in mind that constructivism is not, and could not be, a pedagogical theory or approach per se, it is also true that certain characteristics of the constructivist-based classroom can be identified. For example, Grennon Brooks and Brooks (1993) and Kaufman and Grennon Brooks (1996) have identified eight characteristics that have been observed in constructivist classrooms:

1. Use raw data and primary sources, along with manipulative, interactive, and physical materials.
2. When framing tasks, use cognitive terminology, such as *classify, analyze, predict, create,* and so on.
3. Allow student thinking to drive lessons. Shift instructional strategies or alter content based on student responses.
4. Inquire about students' understandings of concepts before sharing your own understandings of those concepts.
5. Ask open-ended questions of students and encourage students to ask questions of others.
6. Seek elaboration of students' initial responses.
7. Engage students in experiences that might engender contradictions to students' initial hypotheses and then encourage a discussion.
8. Provide time for students to construct relationships and create metaphors. (Kaufman & Grennon Brooks, 1996, p. 235)

These characteristics function both as descriptive and normative attributes in that they not only have been observed in practice but also have been used for evaluation purposes. It is important to note here, incidentally, "Many of these attributes are not unique to constructivist teaching but are representative of good teaching in general"

(Kaufman & Grennon Brooks, 1996, p. 235)—a point that would seem to confirm von Glasersfeld's (1995a) claim, "Constructivism does not claim to have made earth-shaking inventions in the area of education; it merely claims to provide a solid conceptual basis for some of the things that, until now, inspired teachers had to do without theoretical foundation" (p. 15). Furthermore, although it is the case that "constructivist principles of learning do not automatically engender principles of teaching . . . [because] learners construct meaning on their own terms no matter what teachers do," (Winitzky & Kauchak, 1997, p. 62), it is also true that,

> Constructivist theorists would maintain . . . that learning is better or more effective when teachers use constructivist teaching methods, like culturing and keying bacteria as opposed to lecturing about bacteria. Constructivist teaching typically involves more student-centered, active learning experiences, more student-student and student-teacher interaction, and more work with concrete materials and in solving realistic problems. . . Nevertheless, students still create their own meanings based on the interaction of their prior knowledge with instruction, and the meanings they make may not be the ones the teacher had in mind, no matter how constructivist the instruction. . . Teachers create constructivist learning experiences for students based necessarily on what they, the teachers, find salient. But what is salient to the teacher is not necessarily so to the learner. (Winitzky & Kauchak, 1997, pp. 62-63)

Constructivist epistemology has, then, clear implications for classroom practice, the curricula, student evaluation, and indeed virtually all aspects of the teaching/learning process (see Henning, 1995; Zietsman, 1996). Although not explicitly discussed in this chapter, constructivist epistemology also has the potential to affect in significant ways the preparation of teachers (see Condon, Clyde, Kyle, & Hovda, 1993; Rainer & Guyton, 1994; Richardson, 1997a) and the challenge of preparing such educators to engage in reflective and analytic classroom practice (see Parker, 1997; Richards & Lockhart, 1994; Zeichner & Liston, 1996). As von Glasersfeld (1989) has argued,

> Good teachers . . . have practiced much of what is suggested here, without the benefit of an explicit theory of knowing. Their

approach was intuitive and successful, and this exposition will not present anything to change their ways. But by supplying a theoretical foundation that seems compatible with what has worked in the past, constructivism may provide the thousands of less intuitive educators an accessible way to improve their methods of instruction. (p. 138)

The ultimate purpose of taking constructivist epistemology seriously in education, though, is helping teachers learn to empower students to take control of and responsibility for aspects of their own learning.

Propositions for Reflection and Consideration

1. The development of innovative, transformative curricular and instructional approaches in the classroom is an essential component of reflective practice.
2. Thematic approaches to curricular content are often common elements of innovative curricular efforts, as are approaches that seek to integrate different subject matter areas.
3. In developing transformative curricula, it is essential that teachers go beyond traditional teaching methods and materials. Textbooks, for instance, should, at best, be seen as points of departure for the curriculum, rather than as curricular guides themselves.
4. The distinction between curriculum and instruction is, at best, misleading; a symbiotic relationship exists between them that the teacher must take into account.
5. The development of novel and innovative curricular and instructional approaches will often receive considerable resistance from colleagues, administrators, parents, and students. Such resistance can take a variety of forms, including academic arguments, arguments about student abilities, political challenges, and personal attacks.
6. Approaches to teaching and learning that are grounded in constructivist epistemology will be based on the assumption not only that learning is constructed but also that the learning process is a personal and individual one, that learning is an active process, that learning is collaborative in nature, and that all learning is situated.

TRANSFORMATIONAL LEADERSHIP IN THE SCHOOL

THE TEACHER AS LEADER

As for the best leaders,
the people do not notice their existence.
The next best,
the people honor and praise.
The next, people fear
and the next the people hate.
When the best leader's work is done,
the people say, we did it ourselves.

Lao-Tzu, 6th century B.C.

The relations of most leaders is transactional—leaders
approach followers with an eye to exchanging one thing
for another: jobs for votes. . . Transforming leadership,
while more complex, is more potent. The transforming
leader recognizes and exploits an existing need or
demand of a potential follower. But beyond that, the
transforming leader looks for potential motives in
followers, seeks to satisfy higher needs, and engages the
full person of the follower. The result of transforming

leadership is a relationship of mutual stimulation and evaluation that converts followers into leaders and may convert leaders into moral agents.

James MacGregor Burns (1979, p. 4)

THE ORGANIZATIONAL CONTEXT OF LEADERSHIP

The Case of John Dewey Junior High School

John Dewey Junior High School has a student body of 1,000 students. Once the city's premier junior high school, it is located in a lower- to middle-class, urban neighborhood. On entering the school, we are immersed in student activity in the halls as students pass to their next class—students joshing one another loudly, boys and girls talking animatedly in groups, couples holding hands, and one or two couples embracing next to their open lockers. A buzzer sounds. Students race to their next class. We ask one student for directions to the principal's office. She takes time to lead us to the office, where we are welcomed by the secretary and the school principal, who are working on an attendance report. The principal asks the secretary to bring us coffee. We are told that we may move freely around the school, visit any classroom we wish, and talk with any of the students, teachers, or other staff. The principal expresses great pride in the amount of autonomy the faculty have in developing their unique approaches to teaching. He informs us that, at the last faculty meeting, the staff discussed our visit and decided that we should be part of a typical school day at Dewey Junior High School. No special plans have been made. The principal tells us that staff morale is high and that the faculty members relate well with one another. We are given a class schedule and a floor plan of classrooms, and we become part of John Dewey Junior High School for a day.

Not only do teachers relate well with one another, but they relate well with students as well. Students are relatively uninhibited and unencumbered with social protocol. They converse easily, not only with each other but also with their teachers, even during formal lectures. Several even seek us out to talk about how they feel about being a student at Dewey. Teachers maintain friendly relations with their students, creating a very informal climate. Even though behavior at times seems to interfere with instruction, teachers are willing to warn some students repeatedly rather than discipline them and risk breaking the friendly atmosphere. In the faculty lounge, teachers talk about a wide variety of social events. Conversation is at a high pitch, preventing some teachers from meeting together quietly. Laughter is continual. When we question several teachers about how they use their autonomy, we are told about how well they work together and about how that allows them to develop challenging classroom instruction. Because it is Friday, we are invited by the teachers to join them and their administrators at a local bar after the school day is over.

As we walk around the school, observing classrooms, we see that instruction is being carried out in most cases by teachers standing at the front of the classroom, lecturing, asking questions, and assigning seat work even though we have been told that teachers at Dewey demonstrate "unique approaches to teaching and learning." We do see some large-group instruction, some attempts at collaborative learning, and some situations where students are allowed to work alone or in small groups, although these are by far the minority of cases that we observe. Overall, the school seems to be moving in many different directions in a leisurely fashion. With little real challenge from the teachers, students have adapted themselves to the pace of the school culture. Textbooks remain the basic instructional tool used by teachers, but within the framework provided by the textbooks, their teaching is marked by discretion to do as they please. Relatively few teachers at Dewey Junior High School are new. When asked about the seniority of the faculty, one teacher candidly states, "No one wants to leave Dewey because we are professional teachers who have the academic freedom to do pretty much what we want in our classrooms. We are a veteran staff that works well together, one that the administration leaves alone. The principal observes us once a year and schedules a 1-hour faculty meeting once a month. Our only problem is that the students could be brighter, but then, you have to look at the neighborhood they come from. I can't think of another school in which I'd rather teach."

The Case of Horace Mann Elementary School

Across town, Horace Mann Elementary School, with an enrollment of 650 students, is located in an upper-middle-class suburb of the city. As we enter the school, the office is easy to find. The halls, void of teachers and students, are silent. Classroom doors are closed. Inside the office, two students with tears and concern in their eyes sit on a wooden bench opposite the counter, clearly waiting for the principal. The secretary ushers us into the inner office, and we are welcomed by the principal. "At Horace Mann Elementary School, students know that they must study hard to meet the standards of the school and that they have to behave according to the school conduct code," says the principal. "The teachers work hard to teach the curriculum and maintain orderly classrooms." A preplanned schedule of visits to particular teachers is handed to us, and we are warned to keep to the schedule because the teachers are expecting us and have planned special programs.

As we walk down the halls, a few children are standing quietly outside classrooms. We are struck by how each classroom is arranged in pretty much the same way—desks in rows, teachers and teachers' desks in front, and the school rules and classroom schedules posted on the right side of the chalkboard under the American flag. After visiting two classrooms, we accompany a teacher to recess duty, where we watch third-, fourth-, and fifth-grade students explode onto the playground. We go to the teacher's room for a cup of coffee, with hopes of entering into conversation with teachers not on recess duty. Only two teachers are present: one absorbed in correcting papers, and the other reading the newspaper. The other teachers have remained in their classrooms or are meeting with the principal. No effort is made to talk to us.

After recess, our schedule takes us to the classrooms of two fifth-grade teachers. Both not only use the same textbooks but also share an essentially "lecture-test" approach to learning. As we leave the second classroom, the teacher comes up to us and says, "The entire curriculum for all grades has been organized and structured by the principal so that he knows what is being taught in every classroom. At the first faculty meeting of each school year, curriculum materials and subject schedules, developed by the principal and central office supervisors, are handed out and explained by the principal." "How does the principal ensure that teachers follow the rigid routine?" we inquire. "Every Friday, lesson plans for the following week must be turned in to the principal for review before the teachers can leave for the weekend. Moreover, the teacher evaluation system implemented by central office supervisors reinforces the principal's judgments and actions," replies the teacher. In the classrooms we have visited, students have been quiet, attentive, and focused on their school work. Students have little opportunity to leave their seats and move around a classroom. Misbehavior is dealt with quickly; if a student does not obey a warning, she or he is either sent to stand in the hall or to the office to see the principal, depending on the severity of the behavior. Most teachers are friendly and show both warmth and concern for their students, but nevertheless they manage to keep tight control of their classrooms.

We leave Horace Mann Elementary School at the conclusion of the day with several teachers. They remark that they think teaching at Horace Mann is little more than just classroom teaching. The principal's procedures and program are to be followed to the letter. When teachers have suggested changes in curriculum to the principal, they have been told to keep to the program of study because it prepares students in the basics, which is what the parents want. When one teacher used several reading texts in addition to the basal text, she was transferred at the end of the year to a less desirable school. The teachers we are talking with indicate that they have learned their lesson from this.

Analysis and Discussion. The two case studies are interesting because the faculties and principals of both schools, if asked, would consider their schools to be effective, as do teachers and administrators in most schools in the United States. Although the two schools are in the same school district, they are obviously quite different philosophically. John Dewey Junior High School is organized to meet the individual needs of the teachers, whereas Horace Mann Elementary School focuses on the organizational goals set by the principal.

John Dewey Junior High School is an easygoing school in which students and teachers are left pretty much to themselves. A wide range of student behavior is permitted in the corridors. Other than using the same textbooks, individual teachers have a great deal of autonomy in developing their individual instructional programs. Some faculty members have clearly used that autonomy to become highly effective classroom teachers. On the whole, however, high academic expectations do not appear to be held for the students, and teachers have not used their autonomy to study the possibility of developing a challenging middle school program. Monthly faculty meetings are endured rather than perceived as an opportunity for

teachers to come together to discuss crucial educational issues affecting their students. The principal perceives the school as staffed by
professionals who do not need to be challenged to use their autonomy
and capabilities to restructure Dewey Junior High School; consequently, supervision is marked by a nondirective approach. Teachers
like one another at John Dewey. Although they have developed a high
degree of positive interpersonal relationships both inside and outside
the school, they cannot be said to have been as successful in carrying
out a challenging educational program.

Horace Mann Elementary School is a demanding, highly structured school. Parents whose children attend the school know that
their children go to school and learn. They also believe, as does the
principal, that this is made possible by the school's emphasis on
behaving according to the rules of the school. To meet the high expectations parents have for their children, teachers implement a rigorous
instructional program in their classrooms that has been designed by
the principal. Classrooms are well organized, with desks in neat
rows. Children are quiet at Horace Mann and know what happens to
them when they misbehave. Similarly, teachers know that they are
expected to carry out the curriculum as approved by the principal.
Supervision is directive and carried out directly by the principal,
whose efforts are supported by the central administration. Communication among the teachers is uncommon; they come to school in the
morning, teach the children assigned to their classrooms, and then
leave for home. Although the teachers focus on instruction by implementing a regimented program, they do not themselves really participate in the development of the educational program for their
classrooms or the school. As was the case with John Dewey Junior
High School, Horace Mann Elementary School would appear to be
ineffective in some significant ways. Whatever else may take place at
Horace Mann, it is obvious that neither teachers nor students can be
said to be "empowered."

THREE LEADERSHIP STRATEGIES:
A COMPARISON

Educational leaders, and indeed all leaders, behave in many different ways. No single leadership style, strategy, or approach is
appropriate in all settings; rather, different approaches to leadership

will be more or less effective in different situations. Larry Lashway (1997) has argued that three common leadership strategies are hierarchical leadership, transformational leadership, and facilitative leadership. Although an admittedly oversimplification of a very complex issue, Lashway's model is nevertheless quite useful in understanding some major tendencies in school leadership.

The *hierarchical leadership* strategy, which is the most traditional of the three leadership strategies, is essentially autocratic in nature and tends to be task oriented. It views change as incremental and rationally planned and relies on the predictability of the future and on our ability to control future events and developments. The hierarchical leadership strategy is technically efficient and ensures that accountability is easily established. At the same time, it is oriented toward, and tends to reproduce, the status quo. It does not encourage flexibility and has the potential to lead to bureaucratic insensitivity. Perhaps the greatest weakness of the hierarchical leadership strategy is that it is grounded in a rational model of human behavior and is therefore not well suited to addressing nonrational (let alone irrational) behaviors. The principal of Horace Mann Elementary School in the case presented earlier is a fairly clear example of an administrator using a hierarchical leadership strategy.

Transformational leadership, as originally described by James MacGregor Burns (1979), is leadership characterized by the sort of charisma that can inspire enthusiasm. As Lashway (1997) explains, on Burns's account:

> Transformational leaders were those who got results through persuasion, idealism, and intellectual excitement. They motivated they followers not by offering material . . . rewards, but by convincing them that their deepest interests and values could be fulfilled through the organization's agenda. (p. 57)

In other words, transformational leadership relies on the ability of a leader to inspire and motivate others on the basis of shared core values. A good way to visualize such leadership is to recall Martin Luther King, Jr.'s "I Have a Dream" speech. Leadership of this sort can be very powerful, especially in terms of providing a vision for the future. Kenneth Leithwood (1993) has provided a summary of the relevant research on transformational leadership, in which he identifies six core characteristics of such leaders. Transformational leaders:

1. Take the leading role in identifying and articulating an *organizational vision*
2. Foster the acceptance of *group goals*
3. Convey high *performance expectations*
4. Provide *appropriate models*
5. Provide *intellectual stimulation*
6. Develop a *strong school culture*— in particular, reinforcing values that emphasize service to students, continual professional learning, and collaborative problem solving

Transformational leadership also has its limitations, though, in that it requires exceptional traits in the leader, is very difficult to sustain over time, can create unrealistic expectations, and can lead to overreliance on the educational leader (Lashway, 1997, p. 69).

The *facilitative leadership* strategy differs from both the hierarchical leadership strategy and the transformational leadership strategy in that it requires a more shared and collaborative kind of decision making. As Lashway (1997) notes,

Facilitative leadership . . . is explicitly based on mutuality and synergy, with power flowing in multiple directions. Whereas the transformational leader offers followers a vision that reflects their highest values, the facilitative leader offers a daily partnership in bringing the vision to life. There are still formal leaders, but they use their authority to support a process of professional give-and-take. Facilitative power is power through, not power over. (p. 63)

The challenge presented by facilitative leadership is that it requires everyone involved to learn new skills and to play new roles. It is also more time-consuming and makes issues of accountability somewhat more complex.

PRINCIPLES OF SCHOOL LEADERSHIP

Another useful way of thinking about school leadership has been provided by Gordon Donaldson and George Marnik (1995), who have identified three "cornerstone principles" for effective school leadership:

> *Principle 1:* True school leaders enhance learning outcomes for students through influencing others in the school community to take collaborative responsibility and action for their own learning and work.
>
> *Principle 2:* Learning to lead more effectively involves learning how one's beliefs and behaviors at school affect others and, in turn, how this cumulatively influences how well students learn.
>
> *Principle 3:* School leaders learn best when they fashion their own goals and follow their own learning styles, but they also need a supportive, colleague-critic network that is committed to such learning-in-action. (pp. 3-5)

It is interesting to note that all although all three of these cornerstone principles of effective school leadership can be found in schools characterized by each of the leadership strategies discussed, they are, in fact, most compatible with transformational and facilitative leadership strategies. It is also important to note that these principles are, in essence, simply "reflective practice" applied to school leadership.

TEACHER LEADERSHIP

Thus far, we have discussed leadership primarily in terms of the role of school administrators. Such a focus is perhaps understandable, given the typical structure and organization of schools in our society, as Lee Bolman and Terrence Deal note in their book *Becoming a Teacher Leader* (1994):

> What does leadership have to do with teaching? Isn't leadership what principals and superintendents are hired to do (regardless of whether they do it very well)? Some teachers don't see the connection between teaching and leading, and some scholars agree with them. One day while writing this book, we encountered a paper outlining the duties of teachers. It stated flatly that leadership skills "are entirely unnecessary for good teaching." (p. 1)

Needless to say, Bolman and Deal disagree with this position, as do we. Focusing on administrative leadership in schools, though understandable, may, in fact, distort the true nature and significance of leadership in the school environment. Teachers can, do, and must play key leadership roles in public education; indeed, such roles are mandatory insofar as one wishes teachers to be identified as professionals. Leadership is a necessary outgrowth of reflective practice itself, as we can see in the following case study.

The Case of Ana Maria Rojas

Ana Maria Rojas had been a fourth-grade teacher at Longwood Elementary School in Huntsville for the past 6 years, and for the first time in her 6 years in Huntsville she was feeling inadequate as a teacher. Under pressure from the board of education to reduce special education expenditures, the district had moved toward widespread inclusion of students with special needs into regular classrooms. Although the initial impetus for the change was financial in nature, the central administration argued that the new policy was the ethically, politically, and legally correct direction for the district. Ana Maria's dilemma had far less to do with the broad district policy or with the goals of inclusive education in general than with what the policy meant for her own classroom.

In her class of 28 students, 7 had been identified as having special needs, ranging from moderate to severe learning disabilities to students having ADHD. In addition, one student was hearing impaired and was assigned a part-time sign language interpreter who was in Ana Maria's class during the morning. Ana Maria felt overwhelmed by the needs of these students and also believed that she had not been appropriately trained to deal with the array of problems her students were facing.

Early in the year, Ana Maria mentioned her concerns to several colleagues at Longwood and discovered that she was far from alone in her feelings. Morale at Longwood seemed to be lower than it had ever been, and many teachers seemed to be simply giving up, believing that they could really not do their jobs properly under the circumstances. After thinking over the situation carefully, Ana Maria decided that too much was a stake just to give up and that she needed to do something to improve the situation.

She began by enrolling in a special education course at the local college. The course provided her with a good overview of many issues in special education but wasn't enough to help her feel confident in her own classroom, so she spoke with the course instructor about other resources she might be able to access. She also talked with her colleagues about organizing an in-service workshop on inclusion and, with their support, discussed this possibility with the school principal. The principal agreed to sponsor such a workshop, and it proved to be a very positive experience for most teachers who attended it. In addition, as an outcome of the workshop, several teachers at Longwood began contacting and more effectively using the special education staff in the district. In one case, a special educator came to Longwood and was assigned to team-teach with two regular education teachers—an experience that all three teachers found rewarding and beneficial.

Inspired by the changes she saw taking place in the school, Ana Maria also began informally contacting parents of special needs students. She encouraged them to attend PTA meetings and, ultimately, to establish their own support group. She also helped parents learn about their own rights and the rights of their children and to become advocates for their children.

By the end of the school year, Ana Maria still did not feel adequate for the challenge she faced. She had, though, played a pivotal role in beginning the process of change in her school's culture and had become an active participant and learner herself. If she still had a great deal to learn, she decided, at least she was now on the right path.

Analysis and Discussion. The case of Ana Maria Rojas is an excellent example of why leadership is an important facet of the role of the teacher. Ana Maria is, like many of us, faced with a situation with which she is not comfortable. She feels unprepared and inadequate to meet the challenges she is facing. Rather than simply blame the board of education or central administration, though, Ana Maria responds by asking herself, What can I do to make this work? She takes an active role both in directing her own ongoing professional growth and in promoting appropriate change in the school context. She does all of this, incidentally, without any formal administrative role in the school. To be sure, she does not "solve" the problems of the school, but she does succeed in helping herself and others begin the *process* of addressing some issues that are problematic at Longwood.

LEADERSHIP AND FOLLOWERSHIP
IN A DEMOCRACY

The culture of the John Dewey Middle School encourages the professional staff to emphasize individual needs, motives, and aspirations. The various behaviors of teachers are idiosyncratic and do not focus on collaborative efforts. The principal believes that when teachers have autonomy in their classrooms and close interpersonal relationships in the lounge and at after-school activities, a good school climate has been established. The culture of the Horace Mann Elementary School emphasizes the bureaucratic and autocratic standards of the principal and the school district. The principal of Horace Mann believes that when teacher discretion is limited and district curricular and instructional objectives are followed, the school can best accomplish its mission. When teachers meet those expectations, they are rewarded; when teachers deviate, they are punished. It is interesting to note how this situation contrasts with that of Longwood Elementary School, where Ana Maria Rojas is able to help the school community, at least in part, reconceptualize its mission.

In his seminal book *Functions of the Executive,* Chester Barnard (1938) notes that executives need to balance the needs and aspirations of the individuals in an organization with the needs and purposes of the organization (pp. 19-21). The behavior of teachers is *effective* when organizational objectives are met; the behavior of teachers is *efficient* when their individual wants and motives, which undergird organizational goals and objectives, are achieved. At Horace Mann, the behavior of teachers is effective because it is congruent with the expectations of the principal, yet inefficient because the teachers' individual wants and needs are not satisfied. At John Dewey, the behavior of teachers is efficient because the individual wants and needs of teachers are satisfied, but ineffective because organizational goals are not achieved. One school is effective without being efficient, the other efficient without being effective. Although both efficiency and effectiveness are necessary characteristics for a good organization, they are not, on their own, sufficient; an organization might well be both efficient and effective and still be undesirable on normative or moral grounds.

John Goodlad (1984) has argued that, in the United States, schools and classrooms and the teaching and learning that occurs in those schools and classrooms appear similar until the power relationships among teachers, students, administrators, and parents in those schools and classrooms are analyzed. To change the culture of schools such as John Dewey Middle School and Horace Mann Elementary School, the power relationships must be analyzed and critiqued, and plans of action may be drawn to promote change. Otherwise, the organizations will remain fundamentally the same and will continue to be resistant to change. As Sarason (1990) has argued, "Schools will remain intractable to desired reform as long as we avoid confronting (among other things) their existing power relationships. . . Changing existing power relationships is a necessary condition for reaching goals, but it is not sufficient" (p. 5)

One of the most important factors creating an effective and efficient school is its leadership. Gardner (1990) has defined leadership as "the process of persuasion or example by which an individual (or leadership team) induces a group to pursue objectives held by the leader or shared by the leader and his or her followers" (p. 10). The principals at John Dewey Middle School and Horace Mann Elementary School have developed, both consciously and unconsciously, very different power relationships in their respective schools. The behavior of the John Dewey principal might be characterized as laissez-faire and nondirective, intended to create a disengaged school climate, whereas the behavior of the Horace Mann principal is directive and bureaucratic, creating a relatively closed school climate. As a consequence of the different power relationships present in each of the schools, different school learning environments and cultures are created for students and teachers. The environments at both of these schools are fundamentally different from that found at Longwood Elementary School, in which effective teacher leadership was possible.

Burns (1979) has suggested that "leadership over human beings is exercised when persons with certain motives and purposes mobilize, in competition or conflict with others, institutional, political, psychological and other resources so as to arouse, engage, and satisfy the motives of others" (p. 18). In other words, both Burns and Gardner perceive a direct power relationship between leaders and followers, but Burns goes somewhat further, defining leadership as "[inducing] followers to act for certain goals that represent the values and motivations—wants and needs, the aspirations and expectations—of both leaders and followers" (p. 18). Three broad, general types of leadership are identified and discussed by Burns:

Transactional leadership, in which leaders approach followers to
exchange one thing for another
Transformational leadership, in which leaders and followers raise
each other to higher levels of morality and motivation
Moral leadership, in which leaders and followers have common
motives, needs, aspirations, and values (pp. 4-5)

The effectiveness and efficiency of leadership is determined, in
essence, by the "degree of production of intended effects." The leadership provided by the principals at both John Dewey Middle School
and Horace Mann Elementary School is basically transactional in
nature and does not create productive schools in which teachers are
elevated to higher levels of motivation. In examining the relationship
between leaders and followers, Burns (1979) argues that "transforming leadership is a relationship of mutual stimulation and elevation
that converts followers into leaders and may convert leaders into
moral agents" (p. 4). In a school environment characterized by effective transformational leadership, the principal will be able to induce
teachers, parents, and students to work to restructure the school by
confronting crucial problems that represent educational values and
motivations. Once the problems have been identified and agreed on,
both the leaders and the followers are likely to find that they have
common wants, needs, aspirations, and expectations. As teachers and
parents working in committees reflect about the agreed-on problems,
developed courses of action, implemented solutions, and accepted
responsibility, they become, in turn, leaders themselves.

Transformational leadership is crucial for principals and teachers
because so many problems confronting education are basically questions of values, ethics, and vision. All too often, the work of educational leaders in our society is conceptualized as little more than
managing teacher competence and achievement tests, rather than as
helping teachers, parents, and students address the crucial questions
that Dewey and the other progressive educators raised at the turn of
the century: What type of education does public education need to
provide citizens for our democracy? How do we make schools places
where the curiosity of children is challenged? To answer these questions, we need to involve teachers, parents, and students in reorder-
ing the schools so that they become places in which learning becomes
the basis of challenging social practices (see Giroux, 1992b, p. 8). Such
an environment would require educators to be conscious of the values
basic to their pedagogical and political vision.

REFLECTIVE THINKING
AND THE SCHOOL LEADER

The culture of education in a democracy is a culture in which the goals are ambiguous, the context of practice is so varied that it is almost site-specific, and agreement about what constitutes the content of professional knowledge is limited (see Schön, 1983, p. 46). In such a culture, teachers and administrators need a process by which they can make decisions. Mezirow (1990, p. 1) has suggested that individuals make meaning of experience by interpretation and consequently use it as a guide to decision making. Meaning is structured in two ways: (a) through meaning *schemes,* which are "sets of related and habitual expectations governing if-then and cause-effect relationships"; and (b) through meaning *perspectives,* which are "structures of assumptions within which new experience is assimilated." The schemes and perspectives control what we learn. Reflection on prior learning is an "assessment of how or why we have perceived thought or felt or acted." John Dewey, as was noted earlier in this book, believed that reflection should be taught to all citizens in a democracy (see Dewey, 1933, p. 9). Furthermore, he argued that, "active, persistent, and careful consideration of any belief or supposed form of knowledge in the light of the grounds that support it and the further conclusions to which it tends, constitutes reflective thought." Mezirow's concept of reflection differentiates between *thoughtful* action, in which one draws on past experience, and *reflective action,* which is based on critical assessment of assumptions and presuppositions.

Two other useful concepts related to reflective thinking are also introduced by Mezirow (1990): instrumental learning and communicative learning (pp. 7-9). *Instrumental learning* occurs when educators attempt tasks (e.g., developing the curriculum for a new content area, determining instructional methodologies). In instrumental learning, the first step is to assess one's individual and personal assumptions regarding curriculum and instruction. Many times, such a process results in solutions in which other people are controlled and their work areas must be manipulated. Judging the validity of such solutions becomes important. Validity can be provided by two factors: (a) informed consensus regarding the logic of the analysis going into the problem solving and (b) the empirical data about whether the solution solves the problem (what Burns calls the "intended effects").

Communicative learning refers to understanding meaning. Here, teachers and principals attempt to understand what is meant by the language and writing of others. They are trying to fit unfamiliar or novel ideas and concepts into perspectives and experiences that have meaning for themselves.

Kitchener and King (discussed in Mezirow, 1990, pp. 159-166) developed a reflective judgment model, which can be used for better understanding the crucial assumptions that individuals use in problem solving. The authors differentiate stages of problem solving and how the "assumptions about sources and certainty of knowledge" vary and develop. In other words, Kitchener and King actually provide us with a model for classifying the epistemological sophistication of the individual. The seven stages of problem solving (of epistemological strategies) offered by Kitchener and King are as follows:

Stage One: Knowing is characterized by a concrete, single-category belief system.

Stage Two: Individuals assume that although truth is ultimately accessible, it may not be directly and immediately known to everyone.

Stage Three: Individuals acknowledge that some areas of truth are temporarily inaccessible, even for those in authority. In other areas, they maintain the belief that authorities know the truth.

Stage Four: The uncertainty of knowing is initially acknowledged . . . and usually attributed to limitations of the knower.

Stage Five: Individuals believe that knowledge must be placed within a context. This assumption derives from the understanding that interpretation plays a role in what a person perceives.

Stage Six: Individuals . . . believe that knowing is uncertain and that knowledge must be understood in relationship to the context from which it is derived.

Stage Seven: Although individuals . . . believe that knowing is uncertain and subject to interpretation, they also argue that epistemically justifiable claims can be made about the better or best solution to the problem under consideration. (as quoted in Mezirow, 1990, pp. 159-166)

Because many problems that educators face are "ill structured" (Mezirow, 1990, p. 166), it is important that teachers and principals recognize the value of reflective thinking as a process of solving problems, making decisions, and setting direction. Teachers and administrators, however, enter problem-solving groups with different assumptions about what is known and how decisions should be made. Leaders must understand the stages of the reflective judgment model that individual group members may be on, and they must be able to assist the group in developing decisions that are acceptable to all members of the group and that will also meet the goals of the school.

The ill-structured problems that confront U.S. education and schools require the best thinking on the parts of parents, teachers, and administrators. A crucial element in this process is leadership. When leadership is transformational, leaders and followers can work together, elevate each other, and successfully achieve educational reform.

Propositions for Reflection and Consideration

1. In efficient and effective schools, the needs, wants, and aspirations of the teachers and the students, as well as the needs of the school, are achieved.
2. The key to educational reform is understanding the power relationships that exist between students, teachers, administrators, and parents that inform and control the behavior in schools.
3. The same factors that enable students to grow and develop enable teachers to grow and develop.
4. The climate of a school affects how teachers behave. It describes how teachers perceive their work environment. An open climate fosters collegial and supportive relationships; a closed climate fosters a directive and restrictive relationship. Effective teacher leadership can develop only in an open climate.
5. The values and motivations that enable leaders to induce followers to act for goals are the same for leaders.

6. By transformational leadership, a principal elevates the teachers and her- or himself to higher levels of morality and motivation.
7. Reflective thinking is a process that parents, teachers, and administrators can use for problem solving and decision making.
8. Because decisions resulting from reflective thinking may affect others, decision-making groups can demonstrate validity for decisions by providing informed consensus and empirical data about whether the solution solves the problem.
9. School problem solving is enhanced when leaders and followers understand that different individuals act on assumptions from different stages of the reflective judgment model.

PREPARING REFLECTIVE
EDUCATORS

THE ROLE OF TEACHER EDUCATION

Arguments for a profession of teaching in schools must arise out of the special layered context of the work, the complexity of this context, and the special knowledge, skills, and personal characteristics required for the burden of judgment entailed.

John I. Goodlad (1990, p. 6)

The most salient change since 1986 has without doubt been the installation of teacher education reform at or near the head of every agenda for educational regeneration: a hitherto neglected or subordinate theme has become dominant. Just as it has emerged as a commonplace that reform cannot be achieved without good teachers, so it has become axiomatic that good teachers need and deserve a first-class preparation.

Harry Judge (1998, p. vii)

TEACHER EDUCATION IN THE UNITED STATES: SELECTED CASE STUDIES

The preparation of teachers in the United States varies not only from state to state but also from institution to institution. There is, in fact, no single "model" for the process by which one becomes a teacher in our society. This is not necessarily a bad thing, of course: The idea that one can take different paths to become an effective professional educator might well be seen as one of the great strengths of U.S. public education. Different models and approaches to the preparation of teachers, though, will inevitably reflect differences in expectations and standards, as well as philosophical differences and divergent conceptions of the nature and purposes of teacher education (see Goodlad, 1991; Howey & Zimpher, 1989; Valli, 1992). In the case studies that follow, we present four very different kinds of teacher education programs. All four case studies are fictional, but each of the four kinds of teacher education programs is commonly found throughout the United States. As we shall see, each type of program has its strengths, and each carries with it certain problems and challenges as well. As you read each of these cases, it may be helpful for you to compare the teacher education programs described in the cases with your own experience with teacher preparation.

Northern State College's
Teacher Training Program

Northern State College was originally established in 1875 as the State Normal School, with its mission clearly focused on the preparation and training of classroom teachers for the state's public schools. It has grown dramatically over the years and is now a comprehensive college offering a wide range of majors, many of which lead to teacher certification. It has what is essentially an "open admissions" policy, which means that anyone who has graduated from a public high school in the state is eligible for admission to the college. Northern State College serves a fairly diverse student population and is very popular because it is a relatively inexpensive institution of higher education. Most students at Northern State College work at least part-time while studying there, and although all bachelor's degree programs are designed to take 4 years, a majority of students actually take 5 to 6 years to complete their programs.

The Teacher Training Program at Northern State College actually involves faculty, students, and classes in both the School of Education and the School of Arts and Sciences. All early childhood education, elementary education, and special education majors are housed in the School of Education; all secondary education majors are housed in their subject-area departments. Thus, a student wishing to become a mathematics teacher majors in mathematics education in the Department of Mathematics, a student wishing to be a social studies teacher majors in history education in the Department of History, and so on. Courses in educational psychology, philosophy of education, diversity in education, special education, and so on, which involve content that is common to all subjects and grade levels, are taught by faculty in the School of Education, whereas courses in secondary teaching methods are usually taught by faculty in the School of Arts and Sciences. Students seeking secondary certification generally complete a year of general education courses during their freshman year and then complete 2 years of course work in the subject area major. During their senior year, they take their education courses and student-teach. For students seeking early childhood, elementary, and special education certification, many more education courses are required, and students take these beginning in their sophomore year.

Virtually all faculty members in the School of Education and many in the School of Arts and Sciences have extensive experience working as classroom teachers in the public schools. Relatively few have doctoral degrees, and conducting their own research is not a general concern of most faculty members. Rather, their emphasis is on their own teaching and on helping their students become effective classroom teachers.

Most courses in the School of Education involve extensive field work, and the certification program as a whole is basically oriented toward an apprenticeship model of teacher preparation. Both the faculty and the students at Northern State College believe that the best way for students to become effective teachers is by spending as much time as possible in classroom settings with master teachers. The role of the college is simply to provide a context and framework for helping students accomplish this.

Alpha University's Teacher Education Program

Alpha University is a Research-I institution, which means it has a strong focus on graduate education, especially at the doctoral level, and on research. It also has a nationally recognized teacher education program, which is housed entirely in the College of Education. Admission to the university is highly selective, but once admitted to the university, virtually any student is eligible for admission to the teacher education program. The program is a 5-year program, at the end of which the student receive bachelor's degrees and are eligible for state teaching certification.

The teacher education program at Alpha University consists of a collection of university-based courses that seek to provide students with a firm foundation in the knowledge base of teaching and learning. These courses, which include learning theories, evaluation, special education, the school in society, and multicultural education, are taught in large lectures by senior faculty members, who are often highly respected researchers with national reputations. These large lectures are supplemented with small discussion groups run by graduate teaching assistants. Methods courses and other subject-specific courses are taught in smaller classes, generally by graduate teaching assistants and adjunct faculty, many of whom are retired classroom teachers. During the last semester of the 5th year, all students in the teacher education program are placed in public schools for their student teaching experience.

Teacher Training at St. Paul College

St. Paul College is a small, coeducational church-affiliated liberal arts college. Its central mission is to provide a setting in which students will benefit from a high-quality liberal education involving both a breadth of knowledge in the arts and sciences and a depth of knowledge in a particular academic discipline. The college does not have an "education major"; rather, any student interested in acquiring teacher certification majors in a subject area and takes two required courses in the Department of Education and student-teaches for a semester. St. Paul has no elementary education program. The two required education courses are Learning Theories and Methods of Instruction, which are usually taken during the student's junior year.

The view of teacher preparation at St. Paul College is somewhat ambiguous. On the one hand, most faculty at the college would maintain that St. Paul provides an ideal and natural setting for teacher preparation because it strives to be a community of learners committed to education broadly conceived. Good teaching is valued, rewarded, and expected in all areas at the college, and students can gain important insights into teaching and learning by simply observing their own teachers. On the other hand, the teacher training program at St. Paul is widely considered a "second class" part of the college. The better students in each major are commonly discouraged from seeking certification; they are encouraged instead to go on to graduate school in their subject area. As one history professor at St. Paul College explains, "We really don't think that it is a good use of a St. Paul education to end up teaching high school."

Despite this ambiguity, many students do choose to seek teaching certification and are highly sought after by local school districts once they graduate.

The "Alternative Route" to Teacher Certification

As a result of shortages of qualified teachers, many states have developed "alternative routes" to teacher certification. These programs are often designed for individuals who have already had successful careers in an area such as engineering but who would like to change and become classroom teachers. Rather than require such individuals to go back to college and complete a full teacher education program, alternative route programs allow these special cases to undergo an intensive training program so that they can become classroom teachers very quickly (often after a single summer session of teacher preparation work).

Analysis and Discussion. The four kinds of teacher preparation programs discussed are all quite common in the United States. Northern State College is perhaps the most common model in terms of actual numbers of graduates; most classroom teachers working today in the public schools probably were prepared in institutions not unlike Northern State College. These institutions prepare large numbers of teachers and do so in an environment that generally views public education as important and teacher education as a central part of their mission. Faculty across school and departmental lines tend to be involved in teacher education, and communication between faculty in arts and sciences and education is usually fairly good. On the one hand, students have a great deal of direct contact with faculty, as well as intensive school-based experiences. On the other hand, the emphasis on hands-on practice sometimes tends to lead to a lack of concern for educational research and innovation, and it is not uncommon for much of a teacher preparation program in this sort of institution to become somewhat dated and rigid.

The concern for innovative practice and research is the great strength of a major research university such as Alpha University. The overall academic quality of students at such institutions is more likely to be better, and students are more likely to be up to date and current in terms of developments in educational theory and research. Students are far less likely to have meaningful contacts with senior faculty, though, and much of the important teaching that takes place in the teacher education program is done by graduate students and adjunct faculty. More serious, though, is the common lack of serious involvement in public schools found in institutions such as Alpha University. Although extensive fieldwork is becoming more common in all types of teacher education programs, in institutions such as Alpha University it is still often possible for a student's first real school-based experience to take place toward the end of his or her teacher education program.

St. Paul College offers a teacher preparation program that is essentially minimalist in nature. The curricular focus of the college is on liberal education, and specific course work in education is kept to a minimum. The emphasis of the college is on the student's subject area competence, and there seems to be a general, if unarticulated, belief that if one knows one's subject, then one ought to be able to teach it. Although we may have reservations about this claim, at least in terms of employment in public schools, students at St. Paul College seem to do reasonably well.

Alternative route programs involve far fewer future teachers and allow for second-career individuals to make the transition to classroom teachers in a relatively efficient and inexpensive manner. Although such programs have certainly produced some outstanding educators, often problems arise with such teachers being unprepared for the real world of classroom practice—hardly surprising, given the intensive nature of such programs.

Every teacher education program is unique, and the four cases presented here are, at best, caricatures of real programs. It is unlikely, in fact, that graduates of any of the four programs discussed here would be true reflective practitioners, regardless of what the faculty involved in each program might say. Nevertheless, students in all four kinds of programs succeed and become outstanding teachers, just as students in all four kinds of programs fail, either during the program or in the years afterward. Both good and bad teachers can (and do) emerge from any type of teacher preparation program. The challenge is to try to identify the characteristics that set apart good teacher education programs from weak ones, and it is to that challenge that we now turn.

THE REFORM OF TEACHER EDUCATION IN THE UNITED STATES

Calls for the reform of teacher education have become ubiquitous in the last two decades, and significant changes have occurred in the ways teachers are prepared at many institutions (see Fullan, 1993; Goodlad, 1994; Holmes Group, 1986, 1990, 1995; Soltis, 1987). At the same time, much traditional practice remains unchanged— ssometimes to the good, sometimes not. The challenge that faces teacher educators involves the intellectual and conceptual nature of their undertaking. Addressing this point, the American philosopher of education Harry Broudy (1980) made this keen observation:

There is an important difference . . . between the intellectual base for the teaching profession and for the prospective engineer, physician, agricultural expert, or lawyer. These professions have their theory base in generalizations derived from empirical science or highly codified bodies of principles and precedents that are accepted by members of the guild. This is not the case in education. In this field, the important empirical generalizations are very few. Education has to rely on a great variety of disciplines to provide contexts and perspectives for the human encounter we call teaching. For every item that we teach *to* the pupil, there are dozens of ideas, images, concepts, categories *with* which we teach but do not teach *to* anybody. (p. 448)

A further challenge facing the teacher educator has to do with what Bertrand Russell (1950) called the transformation of teaching as an occupation "in the last hundred years from a small, highly skilled profession concerned with a minority of the population, to a large and important branch of the public service" (p. 124). As teachers have increasingly become just another type of civil servant, their individual freedom in the classroom has declined accordingly. This is understandable, perhaps, but also problematic, as Russell observed:

> The teacher, like the artist, the philosopher, and the man of letters, can only perform his work adequately if he feels himself to be an individual directed by an inner creative impulse, not dominated and fettered by an outside authority. (p. 135)

This tension that Russell identified some five decades ago is in many ways found at the heart of many competing efforts at educational reform in our own society: The desire for increased control and accountability on the one hand is paralleled by calls for increased teacher autonomy and empowerment on the other.

CRITERIA FOR COHERENT TEACHER EDUCATION PROGRAMS

In their book *Profiles of Preservice Teacher Education* (1989), Ken Howey and Nancy Zimpher examine distinctive teacher education programs. On the basis of the cases they studied, they identified 14 attributes of coherent programs of teacher preparation that are roughly analogous to the characteristics that have been identified in the effective schools literature:

1. *Programs* of teacher preparation are driven by *clear conceptions of schooling/teaching*. These conceptions can contribute to:

   - shared beliefs, faculty collegiality, and ongoing program renewal

- considerations of curriculum *scope, sequence, integration,* and *articulation*
- to what is valued in a teacher and what is expected of the prospective teacher
- a shared sense of reasonableness for what should be expected of a prospective teacher by identifying a limited number of core dispositional behaviors that emanate from the conception(s)
- more realistic role definitions for teachers through conceptions of teaching that fully acknowledge the realities of schools as a workplace
- an explicit, coherent design for programmatic research and evaluation

2. Faculty appear to coalesce around experimental programs, planned variations, and programs that have *distinctive* qualities and specific *symbolic* titles.
3. A sense of *reasonableness* and *clarity* are associated with the major goals of the program.
4. That the program is *rigorous* and *academically challenging,* that students will have to work hard to achieve, is explicitly stated and eventually modeled.
5. *Themes* run throughout the curriculum, like threads, in which key concepts, like buttons, are tied together throughout a variety of courses, practica, and school experiences.
6. There is an appropriate *balance* and *relationship* between *general knowledge which can be brought to bear pedagogically, pedagogical knowledge,* and *experience designed to promote pedagogical development.*
7. Student *cohort* groups are identified as a strength of the program.
8. At some point in the program, the cohort or cluster of students invariably encounters a particularly challenging element, a *milestone* or *benchmark point,* which sociologists have identified as *shared ordeal.*
9. Organizational and structural features of the program enable an *interdisciplinary* or *integrative approach to curriculum.*
10. *Adequate "lifespace"* is found within the curriculum.
11. Adequate curriculum materials, instructional resources, and information and communication technologies, and a

well-conceived *laboratory component* are found in the program.
12. *Curriculum articulation* takes place between the activities that occur on *campus* and those activities that occur in *schools*.
13. There should be a direct linkage with *research* and *development* into teacher education, as well as into the content that informs teacher education.
14. A plan for *systematic program evaluation* exists. (pp. 246-254)

These attributes provide a powerful and useful framework for evaluating and improving teacher education programs of all sorts. They can also be used to help us imagine what different kinds of "ideal" teacher education programs might look like. In other words, these attributes can give us the scaffolding within which different teacher educational programs, serving different groups and with distinct missions, can be developed.

IMPLICATIONS FOR PROFESSIONAL DEVELOPMENT

The discussion thus far in this chapter has focused almost exclusively on pre-service teacher preparation. This is, though, only part of the story; the ongoing professional development of in-service teachers is also a significant component of teacher education. Thomas Sergiovanni (1996) has argued that if the professional development of practicing teachers is to play a positive and significant role in the process of educational reform and school improvement, such development must do the following:

- Encourage teachers to reflect on their own practice
- Acknowledge that teachers develop at different rates and that, at any given time, are more ready to learn some things than others
- Acknowledge that teachers have different talents and interests
- Give high priority to conversation and dialogue among teachers
- Provide for collaborative learning among teachers
- Emphasize caring relationships and felt interdependencies
- Call on teachers to respond morally to their work

- View teachers as supervisors of learning communities (p. 142)

What is interesting in this list is that each point raised applies just as well to pre-service teachers as it does to in-service teachers. The same point can be made of the six principles advocated by Judith Little (1993) for professional development experiences for teachers:

1. Professional development offers meaningful intellectual, social, and emotional engagement with ideas, with materials, and with colleagues both in and out of teaching.
2. Professional development takes explicit account of the context of teaching and the experience of teachers.
3. Professional development offers support for informed dissent.
4. Professional development places classroom practice in the larger context of school practice and the educational careers of children.
5. Professional development prepares teachers (as well as students and their parents) to employ the techniques and perspectives or inquiry. . . [I]t acknowledges that the existing knowledge is relatively slim and that our strength may derive less from teachers' willingness to consume research knowledge than from their capacity to generate knowledge and to assess the knowledge claimed by others.
6. The governance of professional development ensures bureaucratic restraint and a balance between the interest of individuals and the interests of institutions. (pp. 138-139)

The implicit key in all these principles, we would suggest, is the need to take teachers and teacher knowledge seriously and to provide educators with both respect and encouragement in both the pre- and in-service settings.

Propositions for Reflection and Consideration

1. There are, and should be, a variety of paths for individuals wishing to become classroom teachers.
2. All teacher education programs should be held to high standards, and although there is no single "best" model for teacher education, valid criteria can be used to distinguish strong from weak programs.

3. Teacher education includes both pre-service and in-service learning experiences, and an important facet of the reflective practitioner is his or her commitment to lifelong learning.
4. Educating and preparing future teachers is necessarily, at least in part, a social and political activity and must be understood in this context.
5. An important aspect of all teacher education should be the recognition of the value and worth of classroom teacher knowledge and insight.

TOWARD REFLECTIVE PRACTICE

Reflective teachers are never satisfied that they have all the answers. By continually seeking new information, they constantly challenge their own practices and assumptions. In the process new dilemmas surface and teachers initiate a new cycle of planning, acting, observing, and reflecting.

Dorene Ross, Elizabeth Bondy, and Diane Kyle
(1993, p. 337)

Teachers are expected to reach unattainable goals with inadequate tools. The miracle is that at times they accomplish this impossible task.

Haim G. Ginott

OK, SO WHAT NOW?

Ken Suzuki is a first-year teacher at Willowsprings Elementary School. He recently graduated from Southern State College, where the teacher education program had emphasized the need for teachers to be more "reflective" in their teaching. Although he agreed with this goal, at least as far as he understood what it meant, Ken really isn't at all sure how he should go about trying to become more reflective. In preparing for the start of classes in September, Ken spent the summer reviewing all of his old course notes and materials and even reread some of his textbooks. He felt reasonably confident about his ability to teach the curriculum and, having had a fairly successful student-teaching experience, also thought he could handle classroom management and discipline issues (although these made him a bit more nervous than curricular issues). What he didn't know, he realized, was how to learn on the job—how to engage in the "reflection" his professors had advocated. In fact, after looking through his notebooks, he realized that very little had been said in his courses about what reflection and reflective practice actually were, let alone how one could learn to embody them. So, he thought, what now?

Analysis and Discussion. Ken's dilemma is far from an uncommon one. He is committed in principle to trying to become both a "good" and a "reflective" teacher, but he isn't sure (a) what these terms really mean and (b) how to go about becoming "good" and "reflective." Thus far in this book, we have attempted to answer the first set of questions. By this point, you should have a fairly clear idea about what is meant by the term *reflective practitioner* and should understand how reflective practice is related to inquiry, to ethical issues and challenges in the school context, to democratic schooling and critical pedagogy, to transformative and constructivist curricula and instruction, to school leadership issues broadly conceived, and to the process of teacher education and professional development. In the remainder of this chapter, we provide some guidelines and suggestions for educators who wish to become reflective practitioners.

TOWARD REFLECTIVE PRACTICE

In the first chapter of this book, we suggested that the process by which one becomes reflective is similar in many ways to the description in the children's story *The Velveteen Rabbit* of the way toys can become "real." Becoming a reflective educator, however, requires not just that one endures, gets older, and (perhaps) starts to come apart at the seams as a result of being loved, but also involves an active commitment on the part of the educator to go beyond routine behaviors and patterns of day-to-day functioning. As the Ross et al. quote suggests, the process of becoming a reflective practitioner is, at its heart, one with no end or termination. Rather, it is an ongoing commitment to growth, change, development, and improvement. In essence, the "yellow brick road" of reflective practice, unlike that in *The Wizard of Oz*, does not end at Emerald City, but keeps going on forever. The process is itself the goal.

Reflective educators are constantly testing the assumptions and inferences they have made about their work as teachers. As Donald Schön (1983, 1987) has suggested, reflective practice is, in essence, a kind of "reflective conversation" involving the educator, students, parents, and other teachers. Educators need to realize that their actions as teachers take place in a context of meanings in which other participants have different interpretations and understandings (indeed, different constructions of reality). It is important that these different and sometimes competing interpretations, understandings, and constructions of reality be taken into account to as great an extent as possible by the reflective educator. For example, Ken Suzuki may realize that his setting high academic standards for a particular child in his class may be in conflict with other standards to which the child is exposed in the course of her or his day. Ken, in short, must reflect on the limits of his influence, as well as on his actions as a teacher.

In this chapter, we offer suggestions to help you become increasingly reflective. Bear in mind, though, that there is no simple formula for success, nor is there any guaranteed way in which one can be totally assured of becoming a reflective educator—any more than there is a guaranteed method of becoming a "good" teacher!

The Reflective Journal

In an increasing number of pre-service teacher education programs, journal writing has become an important practice. Pre-service teachers are often asked to write down their experiences at the end of a day of teaching, reflect on them, draw conclusions from them, and share their insights about the day's events with their cooperating teacher, as well as their university supervisor. Many effective teachers continue journal writing and reflection as regular classroom teachers. Sharing is done with other teachers, the principal, and others with whom the teachers have professional contact and in whom they have confidence. In addition, reflective journals can play an important role in analyzing significant social and educational issues that affect students and the learning environment.

Just as there is no single correct way to write a lesson plan, so there is no single correct way to keep a reflective journal. Different individuals will find different formats useful, and each person should be encouraged to explore different approaches and formats to find out what will work best for her or him. In our own experience, we have found that many pre-service and in-service teachers benefit from journals divided into "descriptive" sections and "analytic" sections: In the former, specific events are recorded as soon as possible after they occur in the classroom; the latter is composed after the teacher has had a chance to think through the event and begin to try to understand what happened, why it happened, and what can or should be done next. Such a format has the advantage of involving both reflection-on-practice and reflection-for-practice and serves to link these two kinds of reflective practices together.

Portraiture

Unfortunately, the instructional skills of many teachers are never shared with other teachers because they decide to confine their creativity and insights into teaching to the isolation of their own classrooms. One way of addressing their problem is the process of *portraiture,* in which teams of teachers have the opportunity to observe each other, write portraits of what they have observed, and share their insights with the other team members (see Rogers & Brubacher, 1988). The process of portraiture is especially useful when kept clearly distinct from the formal process of teacher evaluation, although there is an obvious overlap between good, formative teacher evaluation and the goals and objectives of portraiture. This process allows teachers to reflect on the nature of teaching and learning, as well as on their own teaching practice, in a reflective and constructive manner.

Professional Development

School districts can use reflective practice in several ways to undergird, support, and motivate staff development. At Washington State University's Project Learn, for example, teams of teachers define problems occurring in the classroom and then work together to develop and implement possible solutions. These solutions are shared with participating teachers and their school districts. A similar approach has been undertaken in Boston by the Educator's Forum, where teachers are provided with the opportunity to inquire into crucial issues that confront them in their own schools and classrooms. Both of these examples involve reflective practice, as well as collaborative interactions designed to address the "real world" problems of classroom teachers. An important aspect of professional development, as we discussed in Chapter 7, is the need for teachers to be empowered to begin to identify their own professional development needs and then engage in the planning and formulation of appropriate professional development activities.

Action Research

Action research projects, which encourage teachers to initiate inquiry into the problems that confront them in the classroom, is once again becoming an important feature of U.S. education. Nearly half a century ago, action research was a powerful stimulus for change; indeed, it was important enough that, at one point, the Association for Supervision and Curriculum Development (ASCD) identified action research as an organizational objective. Action research, as discussed earlier in this book, can play an important role not only in the improvement of specific pedagogical practices but also in the development of a "culture of inquiry" in the school and of reflective, educational practice on the part of the classroom teacher.

❑ ❑ ❑

Journals, portraiture, professional development activities, and action research are a few of the many ways teachers and other educators can seek to become reflective practitioners. The biggest challenge facing Ken Suzuki (and the rest of us), though, is actually deciding to make the commitment to become a reflective educator. Once on the road to reflective practice, Ken will find many interesting and valuable paths that he can follow toward the goal of becoming increasingly reflective as a professional educator.

UP, UP, AND AWAY?

Ken's concern with the "how" of becoming a reflective practitioner is both real and important. One good way to think about the process that one must undergo to become a reflective educator is to focus on the key features of what it means to be a reflective educator. Kenneth Zeichner and Daniel Liston (1996) have argued that a reflective teacher

- Examines, frames, and attempts to solve the dilemmas of classroom practice
- Is aware of and questions the assumptions and values she or he brings to teaching
- Is attentive to the institutional and cultural contexts in which she or he teaches
- Takes part in curriculum development and is involved in school change efforts
- Takes responsibility for her or his own professional development. (p. 6)

This list is valuable not only as a description of reflective practice but perhaps even more as a checklist of sorts for one wishing to become a reflective practitioner. Again, the most important point that we can make for anyone wishing to become a reflective educator is to remember that it is a journey and that the trip itself is the goal.

We wish you good travels!

REFERENCES

Barnard, C. (1938). *Functions of the executive.* Cambridge, MA: Harvard University Press.

Barzun, J. (1954). *Teacher in America.* Garden City, NY: Doubleday.

Barzun, J. (1991). *Begin here: The forgotten conditions of teaching and learning.* Chicago: University of Chicago Press.

Becker, L. (1973). *On justifying moral arguments.* Boston: Routledge & Kegan Paul.

Berliner, D. (1986). In pursuit of the expert pedagogue. *Educational Researcher, 15*(7), 5-13.

Bissex, G., & Bullock, R. (Eds.). (1987). *Seeing for ourselves: Case-study research by teachers of writing.* Portsmouth, NH: Heinemann.

Bogdan, R., & Biklen, S. (1992). *Qualitative research for education: An introduction to theory and methods.* Boston: Allyn & Bacon.

Bolman, L., & Deal, T. (1994). *Becoming a teacher leader: From isolation to collaboration.* Thousand Oaks, CA: Corwin.

Boulter, C. (1997). Discourse and conceptual understanding in science. In B. Davies & D. Corson (Eds.), *Encyclopedia of language and education: Vol. 3. Oral discourse and education* (pp. 239-248). Dordrecht: Kluwer.

Bowers, C. A. (1984). *The promise of theory: Education and the politics of cultural change.* White Plains, NY: Longman.

Broudy, H. S. (1980). What do professors of education profess? *Educational Forum, 44*(4), 441-451.

Burns, J. M. (1979). *Leadership.* New York: Harper & Row.

Campbell, P., Norlander, K., Reagan, T., Case, C., DeFranco, T., & Brubacher, J. (1995). Ensuring identification with an "other- oriented" culture of teaching: Socializing into a caring profession. *Record in Educational Leadership, 15*(2), 72-78.

Case, C., Lanier, J., & Miskel, C. (1986). The Holmes Group report: Impetus for gaining professional status for teachers. *Journal of Teacher Education, 37*(4), 36-43.

Case, C., Norlander, K., & Reagan, T. (1995). Cultural transformation in an urban professional development center: Policy implications for school-university collaboration. In H. Petrie (Ed.), *Professionalization, partnership, and power: Building professional development schools* (pp. 113-132). Albany: State University of New York Press.

Chambliss, J. (1987). *Educational theory as theory of conduct.* Albany: State University of New York Press.

Cobb, P. (1994). Where is the mind? Constructivist and socioculturalist perspectives on mathematical development. *Educational Researcher, 23*(7), 13-20.

Cobb, P. (1996). Where is the mind? A coordination of sociocultural and cognitive constructionist perspectives. In C. Fosnot (Ed.), *Constructivism: Theory, perspectives, and practice* (pp. 34-52). New York: Teachers College Press.

Cobern, W. (1993). Contextual constructivism: The impact of culture on the learning and teaching of science. In K. Tobin (Ed.), *The practice of constructivism in science education* (pp. 51-69). Mahwah, NJ: Lawrence Erlbaum.

Comer, J. (1980). *School power.* New York: Free Press.

Condon, M., Clyde, J., Kyle, D., & Hovda, R. (1993). A constructivist basis for teaching and teacher education: A framework for program development and research on graduates. *Journal of Teacher Education, 44*(4), 273-278.

Confrey, J. (1995). How compatible are radical constructivism, sociocultural approaches, and social constructivism? In L. Steffe & J. Gale (Eds.), *Constructivism in education* (pp. 185-225). Mahwah, NJ: Lawrence Erlbaum.

Connelly, F., & Clandinin, D. (1990). Stories of experience and narrative inquiry. *Educational Researcher, 19*(5), 2-14.

Cooper, J. (1993). *Literacy: Helping children construct meaning* (2nd ed.). Boston: Houghton Mifflin.

Copleston, F. (1960). *A history of philosophy: Vol. 6. Modern philosophy, Part II—Kant.* Garden City, NY: Image.

Counts, G. S. (1932). *Dare the schools build a new social order?* New York: John Day.

Davis, R., Maher, C., & Noddings, N. (Eds.). (1990). *Constructivist views on the teaching and learning of mathematics.* Reston, VA: National Council of Teachers of Mathematics.

Demos, J. (1970). *A little commonwealth: Family life in Plymouth Colony.* New York: Oxford University Press.

Denzin, N., & Lincoln, Y. (Eds.). (1994). *Handbook of qualitative research.* Thousand Oaks, CA: Sage.

Dewey, J. (1910). *How we think.* Boston: D. C. Heath.

Dewey, J. (1927). *The public and its problems.* New York: Henry Holt.

Dewey, J. (1933). *How we think: A restatement of the relations of reflective thinking to the educative process* (2nd rev. ed.). Lexington, MA: D. C. Heath.

Dewey, J. (1938). *Logic: The theory of inquiry.* New York: Henry Holt.

Dewey, J. (1943). *The child and the curriculum/The school and society.* Chicago: University of Chicago Press. (Original works published 1902 and 1900)

Dewey, J. (1944). *Democracy and education: An introduction to the philosophy of education.* New York: Free Press. (Original work published 1916)

Dewey, J. (1948). *Reconstruction in philosophy* (Enlarged ed.). Boston: Beacon.

Dewey, J. (1975). *Moral principles in education.* Carbondale: Southern Illinois University Press. (Original work published 1909)

Dewey, J. (1976). The relationship of thought and its subject matter. Reprinted in J. Boydston (Ed.), *John Dewey: The middle works: Vol. 2 (1902-1903)* (pp. 298-315). Carbondale: Southern Illinois University Press. (Original work published 1903)

Dewey, J., & Dewey, E. (1962). *Schools of tomorrow.* New York: E. P. Dutton. (Original work published 1915)

Donaldson, G., & Marnik, G. (1995). *Becoming better leaders: The challenge of improving student learning.* Thousand Oaks, CA: Corwin.

Driver, R., Asoko, H., Leach, J., Mortimer, E., & Scott, P. (1994). Constructing scientific knowledge in the classroom. *Educational Researcher, 23(7),* 5-12.

Duffy, T., & Jonassen, D. (Eds.). (1992). *Constructivism and the technology of instruction: A conversation.* Mahwah, NJ: Lawrence Erlbaum.

Eisner, E. (1982). *Cognitive and curriculum: A basis for deciding what to teach.* White Plains, NY: Longman.

Erlandson, D., Harris, E., Skipper, B., & Allen, S. (1993). *Doing naturalistic inquiry: A guide to methods.* Newbury Park, CA: Sage.

Fensham, P., Gunstone, R., & White, R. (Eds.). (1994). *The content of science: A constructivist approach to its teaching and learning.* London: Falmer.

Feyerabend, P. (1978). *Against method: Outline of an anarchistic theory of knowledge.* London: Verso.

Fine, M. (1991). *Framing dropouts: Notes on the politics of an urban public high school.* Albany: State University of New York Press.

Fishman, J., & Keller, G. (Eds.). (1982). *Bilingual education for Hispanic students in the United States.* New York: Teachers College Press.

Fitzgibbons, R. (1981). *Making educational decisions: An introduction to philosophy of education.* Orlando, FL: Harcourt Brace.

Forman, G., & Pufall, P. (Eds.). (1988). *Constructivism in the computer age.* Mahwah, NJ: Lawrence Erlbaum.

Fosnot, C. (1989). *Enquiring teachers, enquiring learners: A constructivist approach to teaching.* New York: Teachers College Press.

Fosnot, C. (1993). Preface. In J. Brooks & M. Brooks, *The case for constructivist classrooms* (pp. vii-viii). Alexandria, VA: Association for Supervision and Curriculum Development.

Fosnot, C. (Ed.). (1996a). *Constructivism: Theory, perspectives, and practice.* New York: Teachers College Press.

Fosnot, C. (1996b). Constructivism: A psychological theory of learning. In C. Fosnot (Ed.), *Constructivism: Theory, perspectives, and practice* (pp. 8-33). New York: Teachers College Press.

Fraenkel, J., & Wallen, N. (1990). *How to design and evaluate research in education.* New York: McGraw-Hill.

Freire, P. (1973). *Education for critical consciousness.* New York: Seabury.

Freire, P. (1974). *Pedagogy of the oppressed.* New York: Seabury.

Fullan, M. (1993). *Change forces: Probing the depths of educational reform.* London: Falmer.

Gage, N. L. (1978). *The scientific basis of the art of teaching.* New York: Teachers College Press.

Gage, N. L. (1985). *Hard gains in the soft sciences: The case of pedagogy.* Bloomington, IN: Phi Delta Kappa.

Gardner, J. W. (1990). *On leadership.* New York: Free Press.

Garner, R., & Rosen, B. (1967). *Moral philosophy: A systematic introduction to normative ethics and meta-ethics.* New York: Macmillan.

Geertz, C. (1973). *The interpretation of cultures.* New York: Basic Books.

Geertz, C. (1983). *Local knowledge: Further essays in interpretive anthropology.* New York: Basic Books.

Gehrke, N. J., Knapp, M. S., & Sirotnik, K. A. (1992). In search of the school curriculum. In G. Grant (Ed.), *Review of research in education: 18* (pp. 51-110). Washington, DC: American Educational Research Association.

Gergen, K. (1982). *Toward transformation in social knowledge.* New York/Berlin: Springer-Verlag.

Gergen, K. (1995). Social construction and the educational process. In L. Steffe & J. Gale (Eds.), *Constructivism in education* (pp. 17-39). Mahwah, NJ: Lawrence Erlbaum.

Giroux, H. A. (Ed.). (1991). *Postmodernism, feminism, and cultural politics: Redrawing educational boundaries.* Albany: State University of New York Press.

Giroux, H. A. (1992a). *Border crossings: Cultural workers and the politics of education.* New York: Routledge.

Giroux, H. A. (1992b). Educational leadership and the crisis of democratic government. *Educational Researcher, 21*(4), 8-11.

Giroux, H. A. (1994). Doing cultural studies: Youth and the challenge of pedagogy. *Harvard Educational Review, 64*(3), 278-308.

Giroux, H. A. (1997a). *Pedagogy and the politics of hope: Theory, culture, and schooling.* Boulder, CO: Westview.

Giroux, H. A. (1997b). Rewriting the discourse of racial identity: Toward a pedagogy and politics of whiteness. *Harvard Educational Review, 67*(2), 285-320.

Goodlad, J. I. (1984). *A place called school.* New York: McGraw-Hill.

Goodlad, J. I. (1990). The occupation of teaching in schools. In J. I. Goodlad, R. Soder, & K. A. Sorotnik (Eds.), *The moral dimensions of teaching* (pp. 3-34). San Francisco: Jossey-Bass.

Goodlad, J. I. (1991). *Teachers for our nation's schools.* San Francisco: Jossey-Bass.

Goodlad, J. I. (1994). *Educational renewal: Better teachers, better schools.* San Francisco: Jossey-Bass.

Goswami, D., & Stillman, P. (Eds.). (1987). *Reclaiming the classroom: Teacher research as an agency for change.* Portsmouth, NH: Heinemann.

Green, T. (1971). *The activities of teaching.* New York: McGraw-Hill.

Green, T. (1985). The formation of conscience in an age of technology. *American Journal of Education, 94*(1), 1-32.

Grennon Brooks, J., & Brooks, M. (1993). *The case for constructivist classrooms.* Alexandria, VA: Association for Supervision and Curriculum Development.

Gutman, A. (1987). *Democratic education.* Princeton, NJ: Princeton University Press.

Hamm, C. (1989). *Philosophical issues in education: An introduction.* London: Falmer.

Hammersley, M. (1990). *Reading ethnographic research: A critical guide.* White Plains, NY: Longman.

Hammersley, M. (1992). *What's wrong with ethnography? Methodological explorations.* London: Routledge.

Henning, E. (1995). Problematising the discourse of classroom management from the view of social constructivism. *South African Journal of Education, 15*(3), 124-129.

Hernandez-Chavez, E., Cohen, A., & Beltramo, A. (Eds.). (1975). *El lenguaje de los chicanos: Regional and social characteristics of language used by Mexican Americans.* Arlington, VA: Center for Applied Linguistics.

Highet, G. (1950). *The art of teaching.* New York: Vintage.

The Holmes Group. (1986). *Tomorrow's teachers: A report of the Holmes Group.* East Lansing, MI: Author.

The Holmes Group. (1990). *Tomorrow's schools: Principles for the design of professional development schools.* East Lansing, MI: Author.

The Holmes Group. (1995). *Tomorrow's schools of education: A report of the Holmes Group.* East Lansing, MI: Author.

Howey, K., & Zimpher, N. (1989). *Profiles of preservice teacher education: Inquiry into the nature of programs.* Albany: State University of New York Press.

Illich, I. (1970). *Deschooling society.* New York: Harper & Row.

Illich, I. (1975). *Medical nemesis: The expropriation of health.* London: Calder & Boyars.

Irwin, J. (1987). *What is a reflective/analytical teacher?* Unpublished manuscript, University of Connecticut, School of Education, Storrs.

Irwin, J. (1996). *Empowering ourselves and transforming schools: Educators making a difference.* Albany: State University of New York Press.

Jaeger, R. M. (Ed.). (1988). *Complementary methods for research in education.* Washington, DC: American Educational Research Association.

Jones, J. (1981). *Bad blood: The Tuskegee syphilis experiment—A tragedy of race and medicine.* New York: Free Press.

Judge, H. (1998). Foreword. In M. Fullan, G. Galluzzo, P. Morris, & N. Watson, *The rise and stall of teacher education reform* (pp. v-xiii). Washington, DC: American Association of Colleges for Teacher Education.

Kafai, Y., & Resnick, M. (Eds.). (1996). *Constructivism in practice: Designing, thinking, and learning in a digital world.* Mahwah, NJ: Lawrence Erlbaum.

Kalwans, H. L. (1990). *Newton's madness: Further tales of clinical neurology.* New York: Harper & Row.

Kamii, C., Manning, M., & Manning, G. (Eds.). (1991). *Early literacy: A constructivist foundation for whole language.* Washington, DC: National Education Association.

Kaufman, D., & Grennon Brooks, J. (1996). Interdisciplinary collaboration in teacher education: A constructivist approach. *TESOL Quarterly, 30*(2), 231-251.

Kemmis, S., & McTaggart, R. (Eds.). (1988). *The action research planner* (3rd ed.). Victoria: Deakin University.

Kerlinger, F. N. (1973). *Foundational behavioral research* (2nd ed.). New York: Holt, Rinehart & Winston.

Killion, J., & Todnem, G. (1991). A process for personal theory building. *Educational Leadership, 48*(6), 14-16.

Kogelman, S., & Warren, J. (1978). *Mind over math.* New York: McGraw-Hill.

Lashway, L. (1997). Leadership styles and strategies. In S. Smith & P. Piele (Eds.), *School leadership: Handbook for excellence* (pp. 39-71). Eugene: University of Oregon, ERIC Clearinghouse on Educational Management.

Leithwood, K. (1993, October). *Contributions of transformational leadership to school restructuring.* Paper presented at the convention of the University Council for Educational Administration, Houston, Texas.

Levin, H. (1991). Accelerated visions. *Accelerated Schools, 1*(3), 2-3.

Lincoln, Y., & Guba, E. (1985). *Naturalistic inquiry.* Beverly Hills, CA: Sage.

Little, J. (1993). Teachers' professional development in a climate of educational reform. *Educational Evaluational Policy Analysis, 15*(2), 129-152.

Ludmerer, K. (1985). *Learning to heal: The development of American medical education.* New York: Basic Books.

Magadla, L. (1996). Constructivism: A practitioner's perspective. *South African Journal of Higher Education, 10*(1), 83-88.

McLaren, P. (1989). *Life in schools.* White Plains, NY: Longman.

McLaren, P., & Leonard, P. (Eds.). (1993). *Paulo Freire: A critical encounter.* New York: Routledge.

Merrill, M. (1992). Constructivism and instructional design. In T. Duffy & D. Jonassen (Eds.), *Constructivism and the technology of instruction: A conversation* (pp. 99-114). Mahwah, NJ: Lawrence Erlbaum.

Mezirow, J. (1990). *Fostering critical thinking in adulthood.* San Francisco: Jossey-Bass.

Mintzes, J., Wandersee, J., & Novak, J. (Eds.). (1997). *Teaching science for understanding: A human constructivist view.* San Diego: Academic Press.

Mohr, M., & MacLean, M. (1987). *Working together: A guide for teacher-researchers.* Urbana, IL: National Council of Teachers of English.

Moll, L. (Ed.). (1990). *Vygotsky and education: Instructional implications and applications of sociocultural psychology.* Cambridge, UK: Cambridge University Press.

Nelson, K. (1996). *Language in cognitive development: The emergence of the mediated mind.* Cambridge, UK: Cambridge University Press.

Nicaise, M., & Barnes, D. (1996). The union of technology, constructivism, and teacher education. *Journal of Teacher Education, 47*(3), 205-212.

Noddings, N. (1984). *Caring: A feminine approach to ethics and moral education.* Berkeley: University of California Press.

Noddings, N. (1990). Constructivism in mathematics education. In R. Davis, C. Maher, & N. Noddings (Eds.), *Constructivist views on the teaching and learning of mathematics* (pp. 7-18). Reston, VA: National Council of Teachers of Mathematics.

Noddings, N. (1992). *The challenge to care in schools: An alternative approach to education.* New York: Teachers College Press.

Noddings, N. (1995). *Philosophy of education.* Boulder, CO: Westview.

Norlander, K., Case, C., Reagan, T., Campbell, P., & Strauch, J. (1997). The power of integrated teacher preparation: The University of Connecticut. In L. Blanton, C. Griffin, J. Winn, & M. Pugach (Eds.), *Teacher education in transition: Collaborative programs to prepare general and special educators* (pp. 39-65). Denver: Love Publishing.

Norlander-Case, K., Reagan, T., Campbell, P., & Case, C. (1998). The role of collaborative inquiry and reflective practice in teacher preparation. *Professional Educator, 21*(1), 1-16.

Norlander-Case, K., Reagan, T., & Case, C. (1999). *The professional teacher: Preparation and nurturance of the reflective practitioner.* San Francisco: Jossey-Bass.

Osborn, T., & Reagan, T. (1998). Why Johnny can't *hablar, parler,* or *sprechen:* Foreign language education and multicultural education. *Multicultural Education, 6*(2), 2-9.

Parker, S. (1997). *Reflective teaching in the postmodern world: A manifesto for education in postmodernity.* Buckingham, UK: Open University Press.

Peters, R. S. (1966). *Ethics and education.* Glenview, IL: Scott, Foresman.

Phillips, D. C. (1995). The good, the bad, and the ugly: The many faces of constructivism. *Educational Researcher, 24*(7), 5-12.

Phillips, D. C. (1996). Response to Ernst von Glasersfeld. *Educational Researcher, 25*(6), 20.

Piaget, J. (1976). *Psychologie et epistémologie.* Paris: Editions Gonthier.

Piaget, J. (1979). *L'epistémologie génétique* (3rd ed.). Paris: Presses Universitaires de France.

Piaget, J. (1986). *Logique et connaissance scientifique.* Paris: Gallimard.

Piaget, J. (1993). *Le jugement et le raisonnement chez l'enfant* (8th ed.). Paris: Delachaux & Niestle.

Piaget, J. (1996). *La construction du réel chez l'enfant* (6th ed.). Neuchatel: Delachaux & Niestle.

Rainer, J., & Guyton, E. (1994). Developing a constructivist teacher education program: The policy-making stage. *Journal of Teacher Education, 45*(2), 140-146.

Reagan, T. (1980). The foundations of Ivan Illich's social thought. *Educational Theory, 30*(4), 293-306.

Reagan, T., Case, C., & Norlander, K. (1993). Toward reflective teacher education: The University of Connecticut experience. *International Journal of Educational Reform, 2*(4), 399-406.

Reagan, T., Norlander, K., Case, C., & Brubacher, J. (1994). Teachers for Connecticut's schools: Postulates, problems, and potential at the University of Connecticut. *Record in Educational Leadership, 14*(2), 27-31.

Reagan, T., & Osborn, T. (1998). Power, authority, and domination in foreign language education: Toward an analysis of educational failure. *Educational Foundations, 12*(2), 45-62.

Richards, J., & Lockhart, C. (1994). *Reflective teaching in second language classrooms.* Cambridge, UK: Cambridge University Press.

Richardson, V. (Ed.). (1997a). *Constructivist teacher education: Building a world of new understandings.* London: Falmer.

Richardson, V. (1997b). Constructivist teaching and teacher education: Theory and practice. In V. Richardson (Ed.), *Constructivist teacher education: Building a world of new understandings* (pp. 3-14). London: Falmer.

Riegle, R., Rhodes, D., & Nelson, T. (1990). *The language and logic of educational policy* (2nd ed.). Lexington, MA: Ginn.

Robertson, E. (1992). Is Dewey's educational vision still viable? In G. Grant (Ed.), *Review of research in education: 18* (pp. 335-381). Washington, DC: American Educational Research Association.

Rogers, V., & Brubacher, J. (1988). Teacher portraiture: A timely proposal for more effective teacher development. *Journal of Personnel Evaluation in Education, 1,* 245-257.

Rosen, B. (1978). *Strategies of ethics.* Boston: Houghton Mifflin.

Ross, D., Bondy, E., & Kyle, D. (1993). *Reflective teaching for student empowerment: Elementary curriculum and methods.* New York: Macmillan.

Russell, B. (1950). *Unpopular essays.* London: Routledge.

Sarason, S. (1990). *The predictable failure of educational reform.* San Francisco: Jossey-Bass.

Schön, D. (1983). *The reflective practitioner: How professionals think in action.* New York: Basic Books.

Schön, D. (1987). *Educating the reflective practitioner.* San Francisco: Jossey-Bass.

Schwab, R., & Reagan, T. (in press). Educational policy and simultaneous renewal: The university, state, and local experience in Connecticut. In D. Imig & C. Frazier (Eds.), *Policies for effective teacher education: Learnings from the National Network for Educational Renewal.* San Francisco: Jossey-Bass.

Schwandt, T. (1994). Constructivist, interpretivist approaches to human inquiry. In N. Denzin & Y. Lincoln (Eds.), *Handbook of qualitative research* (pp. 118-137). Thousand Oaks, CA: Sage.

Sergiovanni, T. (1996). *Leadership for the schoolhouse.* San Francisco: Jossey-Bass.

Sherman, R., & Webb, R. (1988). Qualitative research in education: A focus. In R. Sherman & R. Webb (Eds.), *Qualitative research in education* (pp. 1-21). London: Falmer.

Shulman, L. (1987). Knowledge and teaching: Foundations of the new reform. *Harvard Educational Review, 57*(1), 1-22.

Silberman, C. (1971). *Crisis in the classroom.* New York: Random House.

Sinclair, H., Berthoud, I., Gerard, J. & Venesiano, E. (1985). Constructivisme et psycholinguistique génétique. *Archives de Psychologie, 53*(204), 37-60.

Sizer, T. (1984). *Horace's compromise: The dilemma of the American high school.* Boston: Houghton Mifflin.

Soltis, J. F. (Ed.). (1987). *Reforming teacher education: The impact of the Holmes Group report.* New York: Teachers College Press.

Sparks-Langer, G., & Colton, A. (1991). Synthesis of research on teachers' reflective thinking. *Educational Leadership, 48*(6), 37-44.

Spivey, N. (1997). *The constructivist metaphor: Reading, writing, and the making of meaning.* San Diego: Academic Press.

Spradley, J. (1980). *Participant observation.* New York: Holt, Rinehart & Winston.

Starr, P. (1982). *The social transformation of American medicine.* New York: Basic Books.

Steffe, L., Cobb, P., & von Glasersfeld, E. (1988). *Construction of arithmetical meanings and strategies.* New York/Berlin: Springer-Verlag.

Steffe, L., & Gale, J. (Eds.). (1995). *Constructivism in education.* Mahwah, NJ: Lawrence Erlbaum.

Stevens, R. (1983). *Law school: Legal education in America from the 1850s to the 1980s.* Chapel Hill: University of North Carolina Press.

Strike, K., Haller, E., & Soltis, J. (1988). *The ethics of school administration.* New York: Teachers College Press.

Strike, K., & Soltis, J. (1992). *The ethics of teaching* (2nd ed.). New York: Teachers College Press.

Teal, S., & Reagan, G. (1973). Educational goals. In J. Frymier (Ed.), *A school for tomorrow* (pp. 37-84). Berkeley, CA: McCutchan.

Tobin, K. (Ed.). (1993). *The practice of constructivism in science education.* Mahwah, NJ: Lawrence Erlbaum.

Totten, W. F. (1970). *The power of community education.* Midland, MI: Pendell.

Toulmin, S. (1968). *An examination of the place of reason in ethics.* Cambridge, UK: Cambridge University Press.

Valdés, G., Lozano, A., & García-Moya, R. (Eds.). (1981). *Teaching Spanish to the Hispanic bilingual: Issues, aims, and methods.* New York: Teachers College Press.

Valli, L. (Ed.). (1992). *Reflective teacher education: Cases and critiques.* Albany: State University of New York Press.

Vandenberg, D. (1983). *Human rights in education.* New York: Philosophical Library.

Van Doren, M. (1959). *Liberal education.* Boston: Beacon.

Van Manen, J. (1977). Linking ways of knowing with ways of being practical. *Curriculum Inquiry, 6,* 205-208.

von Glasersfeld, E. (1984). An introduction to radical constructivism. In P. Watzlawick (Ed.), *The invented reality: How do we know what we believe we know?* (pp. 17-40). New York: Norton.

von Glasersfeld, E. (1989). Cognition, construction of knowledge, and teaching. *Synthese, 80*(1), 121-140.

von Glasersfeld, E. (1993). Questions and answers about radical constructivism. In K. Tobin (Ed.), *The practice of constructivism in science education* (pp. 23-38). Mahwah, NJ: Lawrence Erlbaum.

von Glasersfeld, E. (1995a). A constructivist approach to teaching. In L. Steffe & J. Gale (Eds.), *Constructivism in education* (pp. 3-15). Mahwah, NJ: Lawrence Erlbaum.

von Glasersfeld, E. (1995b). *Radical constructivism: A way of knowing.* London: Falmer.

von Glasersfeld, E. (1996). Footnotes to "The many faces of constructivism." *Educational Researcher, 25*(6), 19.

Vygotsky, L. (1978). *Mind in society: The development of higher psychological processes* (M. Cole, V. John-Steiner, S. Scribner, & E. Souberman, Trans.). Cambridge, MA: Harvard University Press.

Vygotsky, L. (1986). *Thought and language* (A. Kozulin, Trans.). Cambridge: MIT Press. (Original work published 1934)

Watras, J. (1999). Will caring teachers improve schools? Various ways to think about curriculum. *Educational Foundations, 13*(2), 73-84.

Whyte, W. (Ed.). (1991). *Participatory action research.* Newbury Park, CA: Sage.

Williams, M. (1981). *The velveteen rabbit, or, How toys become real.* Philadelphia: Running Press.

Wilson, J. (1967). *Language and the pursuit of truth.* Cambridge, UK: Cambridge University Press.

Winitzky, N., & Kauchak, D. (1997). Constructivism in teacher education: Applying cognitive theory to teacher learning. In V. Richardson (Ed.), *Constructivist teacher education: Building a world of new understandings* (pp. 59-83). London: Falmer.

Wood, T., Cobb, P., & Yackel, E. (1995). Reflections of learning and teaching mathematics in elementary school. In L. Steffe & J. Gale (Eds.), *Constructivism in education* (pp. 401-422). Mahwah, NJ: Lawrence Erlbaum.

Zeichner, K., & Liston, D. (1987). Teaching student teachers to reflect. *Harvard Educational Review, 57,* 23-48.

Zeichner, K., & Liston, D. (1996). *Reflective teaching: An introduction.* Mahwah, NJ: Lawrence Erlbaum.

Zietsman, A. (1996). Constructivism: Super theory for all educational ills? *South African Journal of Higher Education, 10*(1), 70-75.

INDEX

Personal preferences, reports of, 66-67
Perspectives, meaning, 129
Peters, Richard, 64
Phillips, D. C., 111
Phonics, 44-46
Physiological (or organic) curiosity, 40
Piaget, Jean, 108, 110
Planned curriculum, 104-105
Planning activities, 26
Political activity, schooling as, 80-81
Political life, 103
Portraiture, 148
Positivist paradigm of educational research, 37
Postpositivist paradigm of educational research, 37
Power:
    facilitative, 122
    principals and, 127-128
    school culture, 127
Practice:
    ethics of care and, 72
    reflective. *See* Reflective practice
Preference claims, 66-67, 68
Preparation, 26
Principals:
    organizational goals set by, 119, 120
    parental communication, 86
    power relationships, 127-128
Principles, guiding behavior, 69-70
Problem identification, 31, 51
Problem solving, 105
    collaborative, 122, 149
    community involvement in, 90
    Deweyan notion of, 20, 54
    rational, 21
    reflection and, 20-21, 129-131
    stages of, 130
    teacher-parent groups, 86-87
Process goals, 24
Product goals, 24
Professional development, 142-143, 148-149, 150
Professional feedback, 14, 16

Professional growth, 125
Professional identity, shared, 43
Professional learning, 122
Public endeavor, inquiry as, 42
Public schools, teacher education programs and, 137, 138
Public statements, value judgments and, 67

Qualitative inquiry, 39-40, 54
Quantitative research, 37, 54
Questions, open-ended, 112

Radical constructivism, 110
Rational behavior, 121
Rational problem solving, 21
Reading instruction, 44-46, 52-53
Reality:
    constructed, 39, 110, 147
    framework imposed on, 41
    negotiated, 111
    objective, 38
    preference claims and, 67
    students experiencing self-contained, 105
    teachers', 105
Reasoning, quality of, 66
Reflection, 1-27
    analytic, 20-21
    critical, 22-23
    decision making and, 21
    elements of, 23-25
    ethics and, 64, 73-74
    group, 54
    in democratic society, 107
    individual, 54
    logical, 20-21
    models of, 4-6
    types of, 21-22
Reflection-for-action, 21-22
Reflection-for-practice, 22, 26, 148
Reflection-in-action, 21
Reflection-in-practice, 22, 26
Reflection-on-action, 21
Reflection-on-practice, 21, 26, 148
Reflective abstraction, 109
Reflective action, 129